One Last Dance

KATIE PETERSON

authorHOUSE®

AuthorHouse™
1663 Liberty Drive
Bloomington, IN 47403
www.authorhouse.com
Phone: 1-800-839-8640

First published by AuthorHouse 9/7/2010

ISBN: 978-1-4520-7100-8 (e)
ISBN: 978-1-4520-7099-5 (sc)
ISBN: 978-1-4520-7098-8 (hc)

Library of Congress Control Number: 2010912752

Printed in the United States of America

This book is printed on acid-free paper.

*Dedicated to the person who inspired me to write this book
and to whom I've looked up to for many, many years.*

Table of Contents

1. A Day in the Life of Gym Class   1

2. I Remember   4

3. The Diagnosis   10

4. The Talk   16

5. Memories That'll Last a Lifetime   19

6. The Final Goodbye   25

7. The Chase   30

8. Come With Me   33

9. The Funeral   39

10. Back to School   53

11. The Ballet   61

12. The Letter   66

13. Plans   76

14. Breath of Heaven   79

15. One Last Dance   85

16. Two Years Later   95

Acknowledgements   99

CHAPTER 1

A Day in the Life of Gym Class

The day started like any normal December day. With the sweet anticipation of Christmas just three weeks away, I couldn't wait to see my favorite person in the entire world, Jason Baylor.

However, right now (unfortunately) comes yet another day in gym class. I heard Coach Roberts blow the whistle. "Okay lets warm up!" Coach Roberts is a large, muscular man standing six feet tall with long, tone legs. He has a bald head and his voice is deep. When you first meet him, he may seem frightening and quite intimidating, but in reality he is like a lovable teddy bear.

"Stretch!" I reach down as far as I can and I feel like an idiot. I'm one of the few in the class who can't touch my toes.

"Stretch your thigh out!" With my left hand I hold my right foot and go into a Zen mode for fifteen seconds before switching and I balance perfectly the whole time.

"Put your right foot out in front." This exercise is to stretch out our calf muscle. Like the thigh stretch we hold it for fifteen seconds and then switch.

"Okay guys, fifteen jumping jacks, fifteen pushups, and fifteen sit-ups. Ready, begin! One, two, three, four…" Coach Roberts leads.

Finally finished, we proceed to pick our teams for soccer. I never was good at sports and really never had an interest in them. Me, I am a singer, and an occasional actor, but most of all I am a dancer.

I have been dancing ever since I was eight or nine years old (maybe that's why I can balance so well) and my teacher and partner has not only been a fatherly figure in my life but is also my best friend in the entire world.

"Gracie!" Matt Stevens calls.

Well at least I wasn't picked last, I thought to myself. As always, I'm put as a defender because it is the least important position in soccer. But really I don't mind because I totally suck at the game.

"Just focus Gracie! You're getting better! Don't allow yourself to get distracted! You can do it! Just believe in yourself!" I heard coach yell with encouragement in his voice.

"Over here, I'm open!" I yell with as much enthusiasm as humanly possible. Trust me, it's hard to be enthusiastic about something you're no good at and don't find enjoyable. However, I had to put forth some effort.

Finally Matt kicks the ball my way. I sprinted down the "field" and gave the ball all that I had, but, of course, I kick it into the wrong goal. Great!

"Gracie!"

"What were you thinking?!"

I heard my teammates screaming at me left and right and I felt like crying. Could this day get any worse? I woke up late, I missed Select Choir for the first time ever, I'm positive I failed my first period history test and now I feel like the worst player in the history of soccer and it's only second period.

I could feel my face turn a bright red and it felt hot. I had never felt so embarrassed in my life and that included the time I went to serve a volleyball and completely missed. I did a full spin and landed flat on my back. I looked over at Coach with tears welling up in my eyes.

"Its okay." he mouths with a comforting smile. Coach was always good at making us feel good about ourselves. He never got angry at us when we didn't do well. He just wanted us to get exercise and, more importantly, have fun.

"Okay guys go on down and get dressed!" he yells, our cue to stop playing.

Down in the locker room the girls try to comfort me.

"Don't listen to those boys Gracie!" says Elizabeth.

"Yeah, at least you actually hit the ball. Every time I try, I fall flat on my face," adds Holly. "Who cares if you hit the ball into the wrong goal? It's just a silly game. Those boys are way too competitive. But then again, what else can you expect from sophomore boys?" We all began to laugh. It was true, most of them were too competitive.

"Thanks you guys!" I replied finally beginning to feel better about the whole thing. When we got back up to the gym a woman was there talking to Coach Roberts and she seemed upset. She wasn't facing me, but from the backside she looked quite thin and her long blonde hair was up in a ponytail.

I just went on with my own business while little did I know the day was really about to take a turn for the worst. As soon as she turned around I knew exactly what was going on and my heart felt heavy.

Her bright blue eyes were sad and scared and she had tears rolling down her rosy, pink cheeks. It was Jason's wife Rebecca.

Scared to death of what I'm going to hear I slowly make my way over to her side. Immediately, she put her arms around me and held me tight. She cried and cried and couldn't seem to stop.

"Wait, Rebecca what's going on? What happened?" I ask with a panic, although, I pretty much was able to anticipate what she was going to tell me.

"Gracie, you have to come to Los Angeles with me right away. Jason's time is almost up and we have to hurry. He said he needed to see his angel."

Chapter 2

I Remember

During the car ride to the airport, I couldn't help but think about all the memories I had of Jason and me. I've known Jason ever since I was born. He went to college with my dad at the University of Colorado and they've been best friends ever since. Of course, I don't actually remember (I was only a day old) but Jason told me the story of the day he and Rebecca came to see me at the hospital so many times, it's as if I could picture the whole thing in my mind.

"It was only a few hours after you were born," he would say, "that we'd gotten there on that frigid November day in 1994. Your mother was asleep and your father's face was lit up with joy. He led Rebecca and I back to the nursery and with great pride in his face and voice he said 'this is my daughter, Gracie Marie Anderson.'

"When he put you in my arms, Gracie, I felt the feeling of protection and love for you run throughout my entire body and the only other time I felt that way was when I met Rebecca. When you smiled at me for the first time, you melted my heart. You had me wrapped around your finger."

I always loved to hear him tell that story, especially, since I don't have many memories with my mother and father. They died in a car accident because of a drunk driver when I was only four years old. Ever since then,

I've lived with my godmother, Melissa Wright, who is my mother's older sister in Denver, Colorado.

~~ ~~ ~~ ~~ ~~ ~~ ~~ ~~ ~~ ~~

Staring out the window of the car, I saw that it had started to snow. I began to remember a couple years ago at Christmas time. Jason was teaching me how to ice skate on the frozen pond a few yards from their house. He went inside for a minute to get a couple bottles of water while I continued to practice. However, I lost my footing and came down hard on my ankle. I remember yelping and screaming in pain. Almost immediately my skate felt as if it would cut off my circulation because of all the swelling. Tears began running down my face and when I tried to get up and put weight on it, I fell right back down like a baby colt trying to stand for the first time.

"Jason!" I screamed, but he didn't come. "Jason!" I screamed again as loud as I possibly could. The pain was unbearable and I tried holding my breath. No help whatsoever. I decided to try and scream one more time. "Jason!"

That time he heard my cry loud and clear. He bolted out of the house and ran as fast as he could. "Gracie! What's wrong!?" he screamed back terrified.

He quickly put on his skates and by the time he got to my side, my ankle was throbbing and I couldn't seem to stop crying.

"It's okay now. Jason's here, you're safe!" he said with a soft, gentle voice. "Arms around my neck," he ordered. With his big, strong arms he cradled me and got me to the emergency room.

The result was a broken ankle in three different places and I had to be on crutches for at least two and a half weeks. Although it meant we wouldn't be able to dance for a while, I didn't care because I knew that Jason would always be by my side. He was my best friend and I loved him more than anything in the world.

rr rr rr rr rr rr rr rr rr rr

I remember the first time I ever saw Jason dance. I was only about eight years old and it was almost Christmas. Jason was dancing as the Prince in the Nutcracker Ballet and it was simply phenomenal. He was so graceful and all I could think was I want to dance. I was hooked on and obsessed with learning.

The first thing that came out of my mouth after it was over was "Jason, teach me to dance!"

He smiled. "I was hoping one day you'd ask me!" was his response.

For eight long years Jason has taught me to dance from ballet to lambawda and disco to ballroom. He has been my only partner and my only instructor and he's the best one I could ever have because he isn't just my instructor and partner, he's also my best friend which in turn creates an emotional bond between us.

There is one time that I will definitely NEVER forget. It was last year on Christmas Eve night and, as usual, we were at Jason and Rebecca's house for their annual Christmas party along with Jason's fellow actors, friends and family. It was always so much fun.

Jason did love to dance but the arthritis in his back and knees caused him to be unable to do it as a full time profession. However, his passion and dedication for acting and singing was just as strong.

As usual (since Jason first started teaching me to dance) we'd created a dance as a little entertainment for everyone at the party.

That year we created a beautiful dance to Martina McBride's "In My Daughter's Eyes" which was perfect because we were like father and daughter.

I wore a beautiful white silk dress that had straps and came just above the knee. There was glitter all over my body which glistened in the white spot lights. Jason wore black slacks and a long-sleeve white dress shirt slightly opened and the sleeves neatly rolled up.

At the beginning of every dance he would always say, "Remember just relax and look into my eyes."

The dance we created that year was a type of slow "free style" which consisted of lifts, turns, and twirls. It was without a doubt the best dance we had ever done and everyone absolutely loved it.

After it was over Jason pulled our jackets off the hanger and said "Come with me outside for a minute."

"Okay." I replied.

The softly falling snow made me feel so light and peaceful. We were so lucky to have that considering that it was so rare for it to snow in LA let alone on Christmas Eve. The sweet smell of cinnamon coming from the house filled the air and at that moment all my worries seemed to fade away. We went out and sat on the bench and when I looked back I saw Rebecca staring out the window with a smile on her face. Something was going on.

"Gracie," he began "I can't begin to describe how deeply proud of you I am, and, Rebecca is too. You will always be my sweet angel and we both love you very, very much." he said.

My eyes were beginning to well up with tears and so were his.

"I know that I usually give you your gift on Christmas morning, but after how well you did during that dance, Rebecca and I both thought that this would be the perfect time." He stopped a moment then continued. "Gracie, this year is special."

I have to admit I was a little puzzled. What was so different this year? Soon enough I would know.

"Turn around and close your eyes." he said.

When I turned around, I felt something touch my bare neck. "Can I open my eyes now?" I said a little impatiently and with curiosity.

"Alright, open them."

When I opened my eyes and looked down there hung a silver cross. It was made of pure crystal with a round diamond at the bottom. In the center was a shape like a diamond of individual square diamonds with a small glass circle in the middle. As I stared at the gorgeous necklace hanging around my neck, I heard the sweet sound of Jason playing his guitar. When I turned around his baby blue eyes stared into mine and he began to sing.

> You don't know how you've changed my life
> On that fateful November night
> When I held you in my arms
>
> With your big blue eyes
> You stared up at me
> From that moment on
> You were always going to be
> My Angel
>
> Your face, your smile
> That I'm blessed to see once in a while
> Your laugh, your love
> A gift I don't deserve from God above
> But you'll forever be, my angel
> My sweet angel

As he sang the song tears rolled down my cheeks. Jason's voice was so pure and real, that it gave me goose bumps every time, and, this time was no exception.

> So many times I've felt like a fool
> For believing that I'd have anything you'd need
> 'Cause your like the wind
> You are strong and it wouldn't be long
> Before you wouldn't be needing anyone at all

But you came to me anyway
And it filled my heart with joy
I thank God for you everyday
My angel

Your face, your smile
That I'm blessed to see once in a while
Your laugh, your love
A gift I don't deserve from God above
But you'll forever be, my angel
My sweet angel

"I love you Gracie!" he concluded.

I threw my arms around his neck and I held him tight.

"Jason! That was the most beautiful song I've ever heard and I loved absolutely everything about it. That was the best gift you could've ever given me." I said with great joy.

"Why don't we go inside, huh?"

With a smile on my face I nodded in agreement. Walking back to the house, I couldn't help but think this was without a doubt the best Christmas I had ever had.

I can't remember a time when Jason wasn't there when I needed him. Through the good and the bad he has been by my side to share in the tears, the laughter, joys and heartache. I thank God everyday that I have him in my life. He is my best friend in the entire world and he's definitely the one person in my life that I know I can always depend on.

CHAPTER 3

The Diagnosis

After New Year's was over that year I went back home to Denver for a second semester of freshman year at school. A couple weeks passed and everything was back to the same old boring schedule. Wake up early, get dressed, go to school, come home, eat dinner, homework, bed and start all over again. Little did I know that back in L.A., Jason and Rebecca were waiting for some news that could change everything as I knew it forever.

Finally the day came. Ring! Ring!

"Hello, Dr. Reynolds?" Jason answered.

"Yes. Jason, we have your test results. How soon can you and Rebecca get here? We need to talk." said Dr. Reynolds.

"We can be there this afternoon about one o'clock." Jason replied.

"Perfect." the Doctor replied. Dr. William E. Reynolds is an oncologist. He has short, grayish white hair, is of medium height and weight, and wears round glasses.

For many weeks Jason had been experiencing fatigue, abdominal pain, and was losing a significant amount of weight in a very short time. His skin also had a yellowish color to it, which meant jaundice, and he didn't have much of an appetite. (Of course I knew nothing about it until weeks later because he never told me any of this was going on). So the doctor ran some tests and finally three weeks later, they were in.

"Jason Baylor," said the nurse "the doctor is ready to see you now."

"Sit down." said the doctor. "Jason your test results have come back and you have tested positive for Stage III pancreatic cancer. Now we do have treatment to slow down the process but there is no cure and at this point it won't do much. It has progressed too much and too much damage has already been done."

"How long do I have?" Jason asked.

"I can't be entirely sure. But I would say at most no more than a year maybe a year and a half." Doctor Reynolds replied. "We can begin treatment as early as next week."

"No!" said Jason strongly.

"What?!" replied the doctor shocked.

"Jason, what are you saying?" Rebecca asked.

"If treatment and chemo aren't going to help much then I don't want to do it. I don't want to have to keep coming back to the hospital week after week for the rest of my life if it's not going to do a thing for me." Jason said with determination in his voice.

"Well there is an over-the-counter medication you can take to ease the pain some and a shot, but, it probably won't do you much good." explained the doctor.

"Fine, I'll do that then. At least I can still do what I love to do. Thank you Doctor."

"You're welcome."

While they were heading home Rebecca noticed that Jason was deep in thought staring out the window.

"Jason, honey, I think you made the right decision. I was puzzled at first but now I completely understand why you did it."

"Yeah, the right decision." he said quietly.

"Jason what's wrong?" Rebecca asked with concern.

"How am I going to tell her Rebecca? How can I tell Gracie that I won't be here much longer? When I sang the song to her I prayed to God that I wouldn't have to tell her that. What am I going to do Rebecca? What am I going to do?"

"Well first of all you know you have to tell her. Second, I recommend doing it in person because as soon as she knows she's going to want you and only you to hold on to. Third, there isn't going to be an easy way to tell her so I would do it sooner rather than later."

"Yeah, you're right. I want to do it face to face anyway. This isn't something I can just tell her over the phone."

❡❡ ❡❡ ❡❡ ❡❡ ❡❡ ❡❡ ❡❡ ❡❡ ❡❡ ❡❡

Three weeks passed and Jason still hadn't told me anything. One morning I was getting ready for school and I turned on the news so I could watch the weather just like always in order to see what would be the best thing to wear. Suddenly, right in the middle of the weather report they cut it off.

"We interrupt this report for a devastating announcement. The beloved actor and dancer, Jason Baylor, has been diagnosed with Stage III pancreatic cancer. Baylor found out about the cancer three weeks ago and has decided not to undergo chemotherapy. The doctor said he only has at most a year and a half to live." said the reporter.

As soon as I heard the words pancreatic cancer, I felt as if the wind had been knocked out of me and I found it hard to breathe.

"No! No!" I kept repeating over and over again. "Why didn't he tell me?"

When Aunt Melissa walked in the room I was sitting on my bed and I was as white as a ghost. "Gracie, sweetie, what's wrong?" she asked with concern.

I couldn't speak. I didn't want to talk about it. All I wanted was Jason, so I just said "Nothing, I'm fine."

"Are you sure?" she asked unconvinced.

"Yes, I'm sure." I lied.

"Okay. Come on then, you'll be late." Reluctantly, I pulled myself together and gathered my stuff for school.

⸻ ⸻ ⸻ ⸻ ⸻ ⸻ ⸻ ⸻ ⸻ ⸻

Meanwhile, back in Los Angeles (having no idea that I now knew), Jason was still racking his brain on how to tell me.

Suddenly Rebecca screamed at the top of her lungs, "JASON!!"

Jason rushed into the bedroom where Rebecca had the television on. "What Rebecca? What's wrong?" Jason asked with a panic.

"You better get on that plane now and go to Denver."

"Why?" Jason looked at the television and his eyes widened. "NO! How is it on the news? I didn't say anything to anybody to ensure that she wouldn't find out that way."

"Jason?" questioned Rebecca.

"What?"

"You've been in this business long enough to know that those people have their ways. However, that isn't important right now. What's important is that Gracie finds out about it from you and NOT the television."

"You're right. Let's go!"

⸻ ⸻ ⸻ ⸻ ⸻ ⸻ ⸻ ⸻ ⸻ ⸻

The entire morning my head was in a fog and I couldn't think straight.

"Gracie, guess what!? Johnny asked me to the Winter Royalty dance. Can you believe it?! A SENIOR asked me to the dance!" Elizabeth exclaims.

I didn't pay much attention to what she had said because all I could think was 'Why didn't he tell me? Doesn't he trust me? Please, Lord let this be a dream.'

"Gracie, are you even listening to me?" she asked quite annoyed.

"No."

"Ugh! Fine be that way!" With that she stomped off in a huff. Normally, I'd go after her but at that moment I really didn't care.

In history class I didn't hear a word Miss Williams had said. When she passed out our worksheet I just stared at the page. I couldn't think straight. Finally the bell rang and I began gathering my stuff.

"Gracie?"

"Yes Miss Williams."

"Are you alright this morning? You seem distracted."

"Yes I'm fine!" I replied trying not to sound annoyed, but I just didn't want to talk about it with anyone but Jason. I wanted him to hold me in his arms and say, "Its okay. Jason's here, you're safe," like he always does when I'm upset and scared.

"Alright then, you may go."

During gym class we played basketball and I wasn't looking forward to it. What was worse was everybody was talking about it.

"Hey did you watch the news this morning?" Allen said.

"Yeah, I can't believe it!" replied Cassie.

"What are you guys talking about?" asked Davie.

"Jason Baylor was diagnosed with pancreatic cancer and the doctor said he only has about a year and a half at most to live." Allen explained.

Although they were a good distance away I could hear every word they said and all hell was about to break loose.

"Alright guys, settle down." Coach Roberts called. "Let's pick our teams for basketball."

Running up and down the court was making me light-headed and weak. I felt my body temperature rising and I broke out in a cold sweat. I began to shiver. It was getting harder and harder to breathe and without warning I started to cry. Immediately everyone was around me like a swarm of bees.

"Gracie, are you okay?" asks Coach Roberts.

I was completely in a daze. "Why didn't he tell me?" that's all I could say over and over. "Why didn't he tell me? How could he keep something like this from me?"

"What are you talking about?" he asked with concern. I felt his hand touch my forehead. "You're burning up."

"Jason! Jason! Why didn't you tell me?! Jason!" I screamed at the top of my lungs.

"Gracie, what are you talking about? Please, talk to me!" He sounded scared and worried as well as desperate.

With everyone surrounding me it was getting worse, much worse. Everything was blurry and I was getting weaker and weaker. I couldn't stand on my own two feet any longer. My chest felt tight and my body couldn't take it anymore. I fell back and I felt coach grab my arm to keep me from hitting my head. The last thing I remember was hearing Coach Roberts scream, "Call 911!"

CHAPTER 4

The Talk

When I woke up I was in a hospital room and it took me a minute to clarify exactly what happened. It didn't take long and once again my head went crazy with the same questions. Outside I heard a familiar voice.

"This is all my fault!" It was Jason.

"Don't say that. You didn't know this was going to happen." Rebecca said. "Besides she's going to be fine. The doctor said she was just overwhelmed and she had a slight fever."

"Jason! Jason!" I screamed.

He ran into the room, the person I was most longing to see. "Gracie, angel, I'm here! Jason's here, you're safe." I began to cry, for I had finally heard the words I was so desperately longing to hear.

With that, he kissed me on the forehead and I wrapped my arms around him and held on tight. I didn't want to let go. All I wanted was for this moment to freeze. Finally, I had to ask the question that came into my head the minute I found out.

"Why didn't you tell me Jason? How could you keep something like this from me?" My voice was shaky and I almost didn't recognize it.

He sighed. "Scoot over." He sat down on the bed next to me. "First of all I didn't deliberately not tell you and, second, please believe I had every

16

intention of telling you myself. I never ever meant for you to find out that way. I don't even know for sure how the press and reporters found out. I wasn't going to say anything until you knew. I never meant to hurt you." he explained.

"I believe you, but you still haven't answered my question. Why didn't you tell me?"

"I didn't know how to go about telling you. You and Rebecca are the two most important people in the world to me. She is the love of my life and you are my angel, the daughter I never had and never deserved. I wanted to tell you in the best way possible and I just didn't know for sure what the best way was."

I was trying to fight back tears and so was he. Suddenly a light bulb went off in my head. "Christmas Eve, did you know?" I asked finally putting the pieces together.

"I didn't know for sure. I had already been in to get the tests done but there weren't any results yet. We decided not to tell you about it because we didn't want you to worry. Do you understand where I'm coming from?"

"Yeah, I understand."

"Good. Now, let's focus on getting you better. Okay?" he said.

Jason stayed with me the whole time and I loved it. This was a time where I was going to spend as much time with him as I possibly could.

～ ～ ～ ～ ～ ～ ～ ～ ～ ～

Within a week I was back at school. Everyone surrounded me asking question after question. "Gracie, are you okay?"

"What happened?"

Coach Roberts quickly rescued me and pulled me away. "Are you alright, Gracie?"

"I guess."

"Well if you need anything, I'm here."

I smiled. "Thanks. You know you can't tell anyone the truth about what happened right?"

"Yeah, I do."

"Okay, good."

~~ ~~ ~~ ~~ ~~ ~~ ~~ ~~ ~~ ~~

The summer quickly came and, as always, I spent it with Jason and Rebecca. Jason and I did everything together. We danced, went to lunch, went to movies, went horseback riding, and went swimming. Many times he tried to talk about the cancer but I said no.

"Gracie," he would say, "we need to talk about this."

"No we don't." I would answer. "I just want to make as memories with you as possible and I don't want any of them to include talking about the fact that I'm going to lose you. It's too much."

"Alright," he said unsatisfied, "we won't talk about it."

From that moment on we never discussed it. In my eyes that little detail didn't exist. However, soon it would be time to face the music.

CHAPTER 5

Memories That'll Last a Lifetime

That time was now.

"Gracie! Gracie!" said Rebecca trying to get my attention.

"Huh? What?!" I answered. I was almost in a trance. I was focusing so much on what had happened in the past that I didn't even realize we were finally at the airport.

"You ready?" she asked.

"As ready as I'll ever be." I answered quietly.

The airport was packed with people who were heading home for Christmas. To me, it was a little early. Christmas was still three weeks away, but none the less that's where they were going and all the hustle and bustle was making me a little dizzy.

"Now boarding Flight 47 from Denver, Colorado to Los Angeles, California!"

"Come on Gracie. Let's go!" Rebecca held out her hand implying that I take it.

"Okay." I grabbed her hand and we made our way to the gate.

"Tickets please." We showed them our tickets and made our way on the plane. Luckily our seats had one right next to the window which always made me feel more comfortable. I had always been afraid to fly ever since

I was seven when I was by myself flying back from L.A. to Denver. The engine had failed and we nearly crashed into a mountain. Although the pilot was able to get control of the plane and ease it down safely, I never got over the fact that it could've been a whole lot worse.

However, today I knew that flying was absolutely necessary. There was no time to waste and driving over 500 miles from Denver to L.A. was out of the question. Flying would get us there in two hours, give or take.

"Ladies and gentlemen please fasten your seatbelts for takeoff." announced the stewardess.

For a long time Rebecca and I didn't speak. I stared out the window and clung to the cross that Jason had given me nearly a year earlier.

"This year is special." That's what he had said that night. I didn't know what he meant by it at the time, but now I did. He knew that it would be our last Christmas together. I shivered at the thought.

"Can I get you two ladies anything to make your flight more comfortable?" asked the stewardess with a big smile on her face. I know she didn't know what was going on but I really wished she would wipe the smile away.

"No thanks." I said really just wanting her to leave. I don't have anything against her but I wasn't in the mood to deal with cheerful people. I was too scared and worried at the moment.

"Gracie." Rebecca said breaking the silence.

"Huh?"

"We need to talk about something."

"Okay."

"Gracie, I need to be sure you are ready for this."

"What do you mean?" I was puzzled. "As much as I tried to forget it I knew deep in my heart that this day was coming." I said.

"I know you did, but Gracie, honey, that isn't what I mean."

"Then what do you mean, Rebecca? Tell me, please."

"I mean his physical appearance."

Now I was really confused. "His physical appearance?" I questioned.

"Remember Gracie, you haven't seen him since August just before school started. He still looked like Jason then. You need to be prepared to see someone different. These past few months he has been getting progressively worse and went into Stage IV pancreatic cancer." she explained.

"And why didn't you tell me this as it was happening? Why have you two been keeping things from me all of a sudden? There used to be no secrets between the three of us. Now suddenly you're taking me out of the loop. Why Rebecca? Why?"

"We thought it was the right thing to do. However, now I can clearly see that it probably wasn't. But, remember Gracie, you never wanted to talk about it anyway."

"I still had a right to know when things started getting worse. I'm not ready to let him go Rebecca."

"I know you're not. I'm not either, but, soon Gracie we're gonna to have to."

I started crying again. After I got out of the hospital I was always in denial about the whole thing and even now I think I still am. The thought of life without Jason was too unbearable.

For a long time we were quiet again. Only about an hour longer and I would be where I wanted and needed to be, with Jason.

"Gracie, I'm sorry I upset you."

"It's okay. I know you didn't mean to. It's not even your fault. Everything is just happening way too fast."

"Oh, Gracie." she said sympathetically.

"It seems like yesterday I saw Jason dance for the first time. It seems like yesterday that I heard him say 'its okay, Jason's here, you're safe.' Now in a blink of an eye, I'm going to lose him." My voice was breaking up.

"Trust me, I know what you mean. As soon as he was diagnosed everything passed too quickly. It seemed to make it harder to make memories that'll last a lifetime."

"Rebecca, you're the only one that really does understand exactly how I feel. You're the only one who is as close to him, as I am!" I exclaimed.

"I know. I feel the same way. But, you know Gracie, we're really the lucky ones. We have memories with Jason that **WILL** last a lifetime. There aren't many people who can honestly say that when they are about to lose someone close to them. So, if nothing else we can at least be happy about that, right?"

"Yeah. You know I never thought of it like that. I guess we are pretty lucky then, huh?" I replied managing to give a little smile.

"You bet we are." Rebecca reached out and gave me a hug. All of a sudden, she started to laugh hysterically.

"What's so funny?"

"Do you remember the time Jason and I took you skiing in Salt Lake City a couple winters ago?"

I began to laugh too. "Oh do I. Remember we decided to race down the mountain and we'd made that bet."

"Oh yeah, um, whoever made it down last had to buy the other two dinner and give them both a shoulder massage." she added.

"And remember Jason was so confident. He kept saying 'Well I guess I'm getting a free shoulder massage and free dinner tonight from one of you.'"

"Yeah! Then we ended up beating him."

"It wasn't a close race either." I added.

Rebecca laughed harder, "No it wasn't. We were down almost a whole minute before he showed up. I'll never forget the look on his face when he realized that he lost."

My eyes began to water because we were both laughing so hard. "I never knew that he was so good at giving massages. I can't remember a time that I felt so relaxed. It was like thirty minutes in heaven!" I exclaimed.

"His shoulder rubs are lethal on me. I get so relaxed that I fall asleep." Rebecca said with a smile.

I stopped laughing and suddenly got very serious. "That isn't what I remember most about that trip though." I said. "What I remember most is that while he was giving me my massage we had a long talk."

"About what?" asked Rebecca.

"Well, I don't really remember the whole thing. Most of it was about things that aren't really important like movies, books, whatever. I'm not sure how we got on the subject but I'm glad we did. It showed that he trusted me enough to tell me that."

"Gracie, there are some things that I haven't said to you before that I should've." That's how he began. "All my life I never felt like I deserved much. I never did anything that made me feel worthy enough to have you and Rebecca in my life."

"Don't even talk like that." I responded.

"Why not? It's the truth, Gracie. You and Rebecca saved my life. To be completely honest, if the two of you hadn't come into my life I don't know if I'd be here right now."

My eyes widened. "Jason, what are you saying?"

"I'm saying that there were a few times in my life where I thought about taking my own life."

"What? Why?" I was in complete shock.

"Because, I didn't think I had a purpose. But, over time both you and Rebecca helped me see that I did and I am eternally grateful for that gift from God. I love the both of you with all my heart." he concluded.

"You know Rebecca, when he told me that I didn't know for sure what to think. I never expected to hear that. You know what I mean?"

"Oh yeah, I know what you mean. I felt the exact same way when he told me that. I loved him even more after he told me that, though, because that was another thing that proved that we were the best thing for each other." she said. "That trip is what I'm talking about Gracie. It's the perfect example of a memory that'll last a lifetime. I don't think either of us will ever forget it."

I nodded and I started to get choked up again. It was hard talking about that talk now considering the fact that soon we were going to lose him.

"Ladies and gentlemen, if you will once again fasten your seatbelts we will be landing here shortly." announced the stewardess.

As we did what we were instructed, Rebecca laid her hand on my shoulder. "Gracie, there's one more thing I need to be sure you're ready for before we leave."

"What's that?"

She sighed, "You know what Jason's gonna ask you to do right?"

I nodded. "Yes, I do."

CHAPTER 6

The Final Goodbye

We got into the taxi that was waiting for us when we got off the plane. My body felt tense as we got closer and closer to the house. Rebecca must have noticed. "Try to relax Gracie. Tensing up isn't going to make this any easier."

I knew she was right, but I couldn't bring myself to relax. Only a few more minutes and we'd be there.

I've always loved Jason and Rebecca's house. It's out in the country so it's always nice and peaceful. They have over 100 acres which leaves plenty of room to go horseback riding anytime. There's an in ground pool in the back and their beautiful house is cozy and warm. It's my favorite place in the entire world and now I was there. Although I live in Denver, here in L.A. with Jason and Rebecca is the one and only place that I feel truly at home because I'm with the two people I love more than anything in the world.

"Here we are." announced the driver.

"Thank you." Rebecca said. While she paid him, I took a couple of deep breaths. "You ready?"

"Yeah, I'm ready."

Hand in hand we walked up the stairs to the front porch. Rebecca unlocked the door, and we walked inside, up the stairs, and into their bedroom. I couldn't see Jason at first because there was a nurse blocking my view. When I could see Jason, I wasn't prepared for what I saw.

Rebecca was right, he didn't look like Jason. His skin was pale and shriveled. He was basically skin and bones and his hair was almost gone. He looked so weak and I couldn't help but cry because the reality of what was going to happen finally hit me and I could no longer deny it.

When we walked in the room he looked our way. He held out his hand and said, "Gracie, angel, come here." His voice was weak.

I sat on the bed right beside him and he took my hand. "Thanks for waiting for me." I said forcing a little smile.

"Oh, my angel, I wouldn't leave without saying goodbye to you." With his other hand he reached up and wiped away my tears. "Oh, sweetie, don't cry. Please, don't cry. It'll be okay."

"No it won't, Jason. It won't be okay. Not really. Nothing will ever be the same."

"You're right Gracie, things won't be the same but, please don't stop living just because I'm gone. Make the most of your life, okay? Promise me that." His eyes pleaded with me.

"Alright, I promise." I laid my head gently on his chest and he softly stroked my hair. "I wish I could freeze this moment and have it last forever."

"So do I baby girl, so do I."

"But unfortunately we can't." I said fighting back tears.

"No angel, we can't." he agreed. He was quiet for a moment then said, "Hey Gracie?"

"Yes?"

"There's one more thing that I want you to promise me."

I knew exactly what it was and I wasn't ready to say that I would. But, pretending as if I didn't know I asked, "What's that?"

"Promise me that you'll continue to dance. Promise me that you'll find another instructor who will continue to guide you and help you get better and better. You have an amazing amount of passion and talent that could help you make it."

I let go of his hand and walked to the window. The sky was dark and it looked like a storm was coming. "Jason, I don't know if I can do that." I finally said calmly, though I was getting very upset.

"Why not Gracie?" he asked with a little bit of desperation in his voice.

"Why not? I can't do it without you, that's why not!" I was getting more and more upset by the second and I began to raise my voice which I hated myself for. "Can't you see? I'll never find another you, Jason! I just won't!" I exclaimed with tears rolling down my cheeks. "I'm not ready to let you go. I'm not ready to face life without you!"

"Oh, my angel, come here." he said and patted his chest implying that I lay my head back down. He rubbed my back and continued. "I know you don't. No one is ever ready to lose someone. But, sooner or later everyone has to. But remember, you still have Rebecca."

"I know I do."

"Okay, then at least think about it."

"Fine. I'll think about it, but I'm not making any promises."

"That's all I ask."

After a while, Jason fell asleep so I went outside for a while to soak it all in. I realized that now what I needed was to be alone and the best way was to go horseback riding.

I headed straight for the stables wanting to ride only one horse, Lightning. Jason gave her to me for my twelfth birthday and she'd stayed there because there weren't any stables in Denver that were close to us. Besides, this was the perfect place to ride.

I opened the stall and patted her neck. "Hey girl, you want to go for a ride?" I saddled her up and headed out across those beautiful 100 acres.

Having the wind blow through my hair as we galloped through the trees helped.

"What am I going to do girl? He wants me to keep dancing. But, how can I do it without him. I can't just find someone to replace him because he isn't just my instructor. He's my best friend and like my father. Why can't he understand that without him there by my side, I just can't do it? No one could ever teach me like he does."

I heard a rumble of thunder and it began to rain. Within a few minutes it was pouring. I raced Lightning back to the stables and put her in her stall. Then, I ran as fast as I could to the house. By the time I got inside, I was soaked to the skin. When I headed upstairs to my room to get dried off I heard Jason and Rebecca talking.

"I'm worried about her Rebecca. She never did take the time to prepare herself for this day." Jason said.

"I'm worried, too. I can already tell that she's getting overwhelmed with it again."

He shook his head. "Rebecca, please, don't let her make herself sick again."

I couldn't get over how weak Jason's voice was.

"I won't. I'm going to make sure of it."

I ran into my room and closed the door. I had to figure out how to handle this. I didn't want Jason or Rebecca to worry about me. Somehow I had to accept the fact that this was going to happen.

As soon as I got dried off and changed, I was back at Jason's side. We didn't talk much but that was fine. Just being together was enough and I soon drifted off to sleep. The next thing I knew, Rebecca was gently shaking me.

"Gracie, honey, wake up."

"Rebecca, what's going on? What time is it?" I said with a sleepy tone.

"It's almost midnight, Hun. Why don't you go into your room where it's more comfortable?"

"No, I won't leave him."

"Gracie, you'll be right next door."

I looked over at Jason and his eyes were soft and gentle. "It's okay. Give me a kiss and go get some sleep."

I reluctantly gave in. "Alright, I love you, Jason."

"I love you, too, my one and only angel."

~~ ~~ ~~ ~~ ~~ ~~ ~~ ~~ ~~ ~~

That night (though I was as tired as I had ever been) I couldn't fall back asleep no matter how hard I tried. I laid there in the dark wide awake. Finally, as soon as I knew everybody was asleep I went back into the room and sat back down at Jason's side. Even though he was asleep, he knew I was there because as soon as I took his hand he squeezed mine tight and didn't let go. I think being in there was what I needed because within a few minutes I too was asleep again.

When I woke up, although the sun was rising, it was still quite early. So, I finally went back to my room and fell asleep for a third time and dreamed about Jason and me when I was little. We were playing hide and seek and Jason was trying to find me.

"Gracie, where are you? Gracie!" he called. "Gracie!"

"Gracie. Gracie, honey, wake up." Rebecca said.

"What's the matter, Rebecca?" I looked up. Her eyes were full of tears. "Rebecca?" I immediately panicked.

"He's gone, Gracie. Jason's gone."

CHAPTER 7

The Chase

My face turned white, then a deep red, full of fury and anger. "NO! NO! He's not gone!" I screamed at the top of my lungs. I ran into his room but the bed was empty. "Jason."

Rebecca came up behind me and tried to put her arms around me but I shook her off. I ran out of the house and headed straight for the stables.

"Gracie, come back!" I heard Rebecca scream.

I just ignored her. "Come on Lightning, let's go." I didn't even put on the saddle, I just rode out bareback. I headed straight for the trees behind the house. I thought I had finally brought myself to accept it, but apparently not. My head was going one hundred miles an hour and all I could think was, 'he can't be gone. He's not dead. I haven't lost him yet.'

We came to the pond where I had broken my ankle that fateful December afternoon. "Woh, girl." I immediately broke down and threw my arms around the horse's neck.

The wind began to blow. I didn't grab a coat and it was chilly out. Suddenly, I heard something behind me.

"Gracie!"

It was Rebecca. I didn't want her to find me. I just wanted to be alone a little while longer.

"Giddy up girl!" We started running again and as we rode the wind whipped through my hair. I could hear Jason's voice singing, "Because you're like the wind. You are strong."

Oh, how I wish that I could hear his gentle voice sing that song just one more time. At that moment, I thought of the perfect spot to ride to.

It wasn't far from the house. It was a spot of open grass with trees surrounding it at the north, east, and south sides. Looking out to the west you could see the sunset which was always full of yellows, oranges, pinks, and purples that made you feel so peaceful. Jason, Rebecca and I came up here a lot. In the summer, we'd have campouts and watch the stars come out. This was also where Jason and I would have our biggest talks. After any performance, we would come here and compare and contrast thoughts. It was also where Jason first called me his angel (at least in my memory). I was six and in L.A. for the summer. We were playing tag and Jason was it. He snuck up behind me and said, "I gotcha! I've caught my angel."

I sat down on the wet grass and looked out at the wide open sky with tears rolling down my cheeks. I knew Rebecca wouldn't be far behind. She probably knew this is where I would be going to.

Suddenly, I felt a breeze and heard a gentle whisper. "Gracie."

"Jason!"

"Gracie."

"Jason, is that you?"

"Gracie it's okay. Jason's here, you're safe. You don't have to worry about me."

"Jason! Where are you?"

"Gracie, honey, Jason's gone." Rebecca said walking up behind me.

"No he's not! I can hear his voice."

"Gracie, Jason is gone. There isn't anything you can do to change that." I could hear the concern and desperation in her voice.

"No, he's not. I heard him say 'its okay, Jason's here, you're safe' just like always."

"Gracie, you only think you did because you want him back."

"I heard it!" I fell to my knees and put my hands over my face. I felt Rebecca embrace me and at that moment I finally realized that she was right. Jason was gone and he wasn't coming back.

"Rebecca?" I sobbed.

"What, Gracie?"

"Jason's gone. He's not here anymore." I held to her tightly and didn't let go. She did the same and together we cried.

"No Gracie, he's not here anymore. But now he's watching over us." She kissed me on the forehead. "Come on, let's go back to the house where it's warm."

For the remainder of the day, Rebecca and I didn't deal with any funeral things. We didn't want to. All we wanted to do was spend the day together. We talked about old times, looked at pictures, and wiped each other's tears. We could worry about the details tomorrow. Today we were going to enjoy each other's company because we were the only ones that truly felt what the other was feeling.

CHAPTER 8

Come With Me

The next few days were the hardest I had ever spent in my life. I didn't have much of an appetite, I was quickly losing weight and I barely slept at all. When I did, it was only for a half an hour at the most because I would wake up screaming, "JASON!" The reason was because all I saw was Jason lying in that bed so lifeless and helpless.

"Gracie, honey, its going to be okay. Shh. It's okay." Rebecca would say as she rubbed my back and tried to calm me down. Although she didn't know it, after she left I would never go back to sleep. I just laid there in the dark and wished that this was all a dream and I would wake up with Jason right there next to me with a smile on his face.

The night before the funeral I didn't even try to sleep. The Christmas tree was already up, so after Rebecca was in bed, I got up and sat in the living room with no light except the glow of the Christmas tree. Beep! Beep! I took my drink out of the microwave. Late at night, a cup of warm milk was always the best choice. It was always so soothing to me.

As I sat there on the couch, words and a melody popped into my head. I did what Jason always told me to. "When you get an idea, write it down so you won't forget it, even if it's only one line."

I ran and got a paper and pencil and wrote it all out. The words steadily flowed out of my head and onto the paper like a waterfall. So did the tears, as I wrote the words which told all about Jason's death. As I wrote the final line, I heard footsteps.

"Gracie?" Rebecca said.

"Did I wake you?" I asked with guilt in my voice.

"No, no, um, I just couldn't sleep, and from the looks of it you couldn't either." She concluded as she sat down next to me.

I sighed. "Rebecca, I haven't been able to sleep since the night after Jason died. After I would wake up screaming from those nightmares when you thought I'd went back to sleep, I never did. I was wide awake."

"Did you even try to go back to sleep?"

"No, because every time I had those dreams I was seeing Jason suffering again and I didn't want to see that. Maybe if I was seeing him happy and healthy, I would've but I never did." I explained. "Course, then again, I probably wouldn't of woken up screaming in the first place."

I could see the concern in her eyes and it made me feel bad again.

"Rebecca, I don't want you to worry about me."

"Gracie, its hard not to considering the fact that you've barely gotten any rest, you've barely eaten, and you're losing a lot of weight way, way too quickly."

"That's because it seems like, in a blink of an eye, he was gone. Everything happened too fast."

Rebecca didn't say anything right away and I knew why. I knew what she was thinking and I knew she was right. The reason why it all seemed to happen all of a sudden was because all those times that Jason tried to talk about it, I refused to talk about it. I kept pretending like it wasn't happening. So, now that it finally did happen, I was just beginning to accept the fact that it was going to happen.

"Gracie, I know this is hard but you can't expect to get through this on your own. Right now, you and I need each other. So, please let me help."

"Okay, it did seem a little easier that day we spent together."

"Yeah it did." Rebecca agreed. She looked at the pencil and paper in my hand. "So, what are you writing?" she asked, skillfully changing the subject.

"As I was sitting out here drinking my milk, a song popped into my head and you know what Jason always said."

"When you get an idea, write it down so you won't forget it, even if it's only one line." we said in unison.

"So, are you going to read it to me?"

"Do you want me to read it or sing it? I have the melody in my head too."

"Well then yeah, sing it. A melody makes all the difference."

"Okay, but bare with me because I've been crying the whole time."

"Don't worry about that. It's okay."

As I sang the song, both of us began to cry. Although it wasn't finished yet, it didn't matter. It was already perfect.

God saw him getting tired
A cure not meant to be
So he wrapped his arms around him
And whispered, "Come with me"

Now he's up in heaven
Watching from above
Gazing upon his children
And his one and only love.
You can almost hear him saying
"Don't worry about me.
My soul was lifted up to him,
When God whispered, 'Come with me.'"

"Gracie I…I'm speechless. That was absolutely beautiful. Jason would be so proud of you and so am I."

"Thanks Rebecca. But you know, when I was writing it, it was for Jason."

"Uh-huh."

"Yet, 'gazing upon his children' came into my head. That doesn't fit. You and Jason never had any kids."

"Gracie?" she asked a tad annoyed.

"What?"

"When are you going to understand? You are his child. You're our child. So, you see, it does fit."

"Not totally."

"What do you mean?"

"That's only one. Children, it's plural."

"Gracie you are so over thinking this. Who cares if it's plural? It came to you for a reason and it fits perfectly. Please, stop questioning it, okay."

"Okay, okay. The two of us understand it, but, will other people? They might not accept that."

"So what if they don't. That's their problem, not yours. You know how much Jason loved you and you know how much I love you. Nothing else matters."

"You're right Rebecca. Nothing else matters as long as I know he loved me."

She smiled. "Hey, I have an idea."

"What's that?"

"What if you sang that song tomorrow? You said that you wrote it for Jason. It's the perfect way to show it."

"I don't know about that Rebecca. One, it's not even finished, two, I don't have the music written which without Jason's help it'll take forever to get written, and three, I broke down just writing the song and singing it for you."

"Okay, first of all it's perfect the way it is and you don't have to have the music written. As far as breaking down goes, that doesn't even matter. People will understand. By writing this song, you've truly shown how much you loved him. Now you can share that love with everyone else. At least think about it, okay."

"Alright, I'll think about it."

"Good. Now, I'm going to go back to bed and try to sleep. You need to try to get some sleep, too. Please try!" she pleaded.

"Let me stay here a little while longer." She gave me a stern look. "Please."

"Okay fine, a little longer." she replied, reluctantly giving in to my pleas.

"Thank you."

"Good night, Gracie. I love you."

As she kissed me on the forehead I said, "Good night. I love you too."

I didn't go back to my room very quickly. I sat there for hours thinking about what Rebecca had said. I have to admit, I never expected her to ask me that. What was I supposed to do?

I did everything to help me decide. I made a pro-con list, flipped a coin 100 times, and even did drawing out of a hat. Everything I did resulted in the same thing- singing the song. My heart was telling me to do it, and I know you should listen to your heart but my head was so not ready.

Then something struck me. One of the things Rebecca had said really stuck out in my mind.

"By writing this song you've truly shown how much you loved him. Now you can share that love with everyone else."

Those two simple sentences were the key to making my decision. I wanted to show everyone how much I loved Jason and how much he meant to me. This would be a whole lot easier than trying to dance without Jason right there by my side. That I definitely couldn't do. Gradually the decision became easier and easier to make. I knew in my heart that the decision I made was the right one for me.

Finally, at 5 a.m. I went back into my bedroom. However, I still didn't sleep because although I had made my decision, the next day was still going to be the hardest day I had ever spent in my life. Having to say my last goodbye and closing the casket was DEFINITELY not something I was ready for, and, to be completely honest, it scared the heck out of me.

CHAPTER 9

The Funeral

Morning came and I was still wide awake so I went downstairs to the kitchen and put on a pot of coffee. I knew that we would need it. Today, we were going to need a lot of energy.

I looked at the clock and it said 7:45 a.m. I still had an hour before time to get ready to go. So, I poured myself a cup of coffee and added a teaspoon of sugar and milk. Then, I went to the computer knowing that I probably had hundreds upon hundreds of emails to read. As I suspected, I had one hundred fifteen. Some were junk mail which lowered it some. But, even after I deleted them all, there were still about seventy-three or so left.

I proceeded to read them all one by one. Everyone was full of sympathy about Jason saying that they'd be praying, and if I needed anything to let them know. I got through about ten of them pretty easily and I held myself together as best I could. But, I had to stop after the one from my Grandma (my mom's mom). It read:

Gracie,

A friend of mine sent me this when your mother and father passed. It helped me a lot. I hope it helps you cope with the loss of Jason.

Love,

Grandma.

It was a poem by an unknown author. As I read the words, I tried to hold back the tears but I just couldn't.

> Remember me in quiet days
> While raindrops whisper on your pane.
> But in your memories have no grief,
> Let just the joy we knew remain.
>
> Remember me when evening stars
> Look down on you with steadfast eyes.
> Remember if once you wake
> To catch a glimpse of red sunrise.

I couldn't finish it. I had to stop reading right in the middle of it. As I exited out of my emails, my ankle began to throb uncontrollably. I looked out the window, the sky was gray. A thunderstorm was coming. I have to admit, it didn't surprise me. I knew the day wasn't going to be a bright and sunny one. How could it? I finished up my coffee and looked at the clock, 8:45 a.m. We had to be at the church by 10:15.

While the straightening iron heated up, I took a quick shower. I got a little scared as I stepped out on to the mat because I felt very unbalanced. However, it quickly came and went so I figured it was just the heat of the water and I soon let it go.

While getting ready, I listened to the music that both Jason and I loved- country. One of our favorites "Traveling Soldier" by the Dixie Chicks played. I couldn't help but sing along. It seemed to soothe me as I ran the iron through my hair.

I heard the shower running which meant Rebecca was up, too. I knew that she'd want to know what I decided to do and I was thankfully prepared to give her an answer.

I shut off the iron and took out my black shirt, black skirt, and black heels. Jason didn't care much for black. He said it was a depressing color. If he walked in a room where every single person was wearing black, he would go absolutely insane. With that in mind, I put the black shirt back and pulled out a long-sleeve red silk blouse. Red was Jason's favorite color.

After I was dressed, I put my hair up in a silver clip with rhinestones and my diamond ring that was my mother's. My hands began to shake as I reached for the last thing that I had to put on, Jason's cross. That's when Rebecca walked in. I couldn't get it to clasp because my hands were shaking so badly.

"Here let me." she said.

"Thanks." I couldn't help but smile when she stepped in front of the mirror behind me. "A red shirt." I said.

She smiled, too. "I guess we think alike. You know how Jason hated black, and I thought, how would being in all black from head to toe, honor him?" she said.

"I thought the same thing. Wearing his favorite color would be more honorable." I added.

"That it would be." We were quiet for a minute then she continued. "Did you make a decision?" she asked.

"Yes I did."

"And?"

"I'll do it under one condition."

"What's that?"

"That you'll stand there next to me."

She seemed to be relieved after I said that. I think she thought there would be more to it than that. With a smile she said, "Of course I will."

"Okay, then I will do it. Oh, by the way, there's coffee downstairs."

"Good. I need a jolt."

I rubbed my face. "Yeah, I need another one too."

When I looked up, Rebecca's face was serious. "You didn't sleep again last night, did you?"

"No, but I promise you, I did try."

"Gracie!" she said a little irritated.

"I'm sorry. I'm not doing it on purpose you know."

She quickly made herself calm. "It's okay. Come on, let's go downstairs."

"Alright."

While I filled up my Notre Dame travel mug there was a knock at the door.

"I'll get it Gracie."

"Okay."

It was Lance, our driver. He's been the driver for over 20 years. After all these years, he's more like a part of the family then an employee. "Are you ready to go, Rebecca?" he asked.

Rebecca looked my way. I nodded. "Yes." she replied.

On the way to the church my heart began to feel heavy. Rebecca grabbed my hand and squeezed it tight. I wouldn't let go for a long time. She gave me a smile and I smiled back.

"Just breathe, okay. Just breathe." she said in a comforting way.

St. John Catholic Church is an absolutely gorgeous building. It's made entirely of red brick and there are stain glass windows all along the east and west walls. My favorite one shows Jesus and the apostles at the Last Supper. Inside, the ceiling is nearly a mile high and is painted a midnight blue. The floor is made entirely of white marble. It takes your breath away when you walk into it for the first time.

When we went inside, Fr. Matthew was there to greet us. "Rebecca! Gracie!" he said. "I'm so sorry about Jason. He was such a good man."

"Yes, he was." Rebecca replied. I could tell that she was trying to fight back tears. She was being so strong through this whole thing. Father Matthew gave us both a hug.

We knew people would be showing up soon because we were going to have a visitation first.

So, Rebecca headed towards the casket. She stopped and held out her hand turning towards me. "Come on, Gracie."

I shook my head. "No, not yet. I'm trying to be strong right now and if I go to that casket, I'll lose it."

I could tell that she understood what I was saying. "Alright."

It didn't take long for the church to fill up. Everything was soon a great big blur. I only knew about eighty-five percent of the people. The other fifteen percent I didn't have the slightest idea who they were but they apparently knew me. It was all a little overwhelming and once again my hands began to shake and that soon spread through my entire body and I broke out in a cold sweat. I could tell Rebecca had noticed.

"Gracie, honey, why don't you go take a breather."

"Rebecca, I can't. I have a duty to stand here, too, you know."

"Gracie, right now, your health is more important and right now you're heading towards the same direction as before. I don't want that to happen again. So, please." she pleaded with me.

"Okay, fine." I kissed her on the cheek and headed outside. Thank God it hadn't started raining yet. I went and sat on the bench next to the grotto which had a statue of the virgin Mary holding Jesus as a young boy.

I buried my face in my hands and I began to weep uncontrollably. I couldn't fight it any longer.

∿∿ ∿∿ ∿∿ ∿∿ ∿∿ ∿∿ ∿∿ ∿∿ ∿∿ ∿∿

Back in the church where the line didn't seem to be getting any shorter, Rebecca was still greeting people.

"Hey, Rob! Matt!" she exclaimed. Rob and Matt were good friends of Jason, Rebecca and mine. I've known them my whole life too. They co-starred with Jason in a couple of films and they, too, were like family.

"Hey, Rebecca. We're so, so sorry." said Matt.

"Thanks. Hey, I'm glad the two of you are here. I need your help."

"Hey, where's Gracie at?" asked Rob.

"That's what I need your help with."

"Why? Is she okay?" asked Matt with a panic.

"No, and I'm worried about her. She's on the verge of getting sick again. She's barely slept at all since Jason died, she's barely eating and she's losing a lot of weight. Plus, she's completely overwhelmed again. This morning, when I came into her room she was trying to put on the cross Jason gave her, but, she couldn't because her hands were shaking so bad."

"Oh no." said Rob.

"Why exactly hasn't she been able to sleep?" asked Matt.

"Mostly because whenever she would fall asleep, within a half an hour she'd wake up screaming 'JASON!' She said that after she'd never go back to sleep because all she saw was Jason suffering again."

"Oh my God." said Matt.

"Where is she at now?" asked Rob.

"It was getting worse. She was shaking again and was sweating so I told her to go out and take a breather. She probably went to the grotto. It's one of her favorite spots here."

"Okay, we'll go talk to her and make sure she's doing alright." said Rob.

"Thank you."

"Don't worry about it."

～ ～ ～ ～ ～ ～ ～ ～ ～ ～

I had to pull myself together but I couldn't. Then I heard a familiar voice.

"Gracie." It was Rob.

"Rob! Matt!" I ran into their arms and began to cry harder than ever.

"Gracie, honey, it's okay." Rob kissed me on the forehead and Matt lifted me up and cradled me. I saw him look at Rob with concern.

"Gracie, you're shaking bad." he said.

Rob put his hands on my back and arms. "Yeah, you are." he agreed. "Come on let's sit."

I didn't say anything for a long time and neither did they, (mostly because I couldn't stop crying). I buried my face in Rob's chest and Matt gently rubbed my back.

"Come on Gracie. Talk to us." Rob finally said.

I finally looked up. "I'm not ready for this. I'm not ready to say goodbye to him. I just can't let him go. I want him back!" I sobbed.

"Oh, honey. We know you want him back, but you can't have him back." said Matt.

"I know that. I can't even begin to explain what I would do to be in his arms just one more time. I would do anything to hear the words, 'its okay, Jason's here, you're safe' just one more time. But, I won't and the thought of him not being here anymore scares the heck out of me."

Matt and Rob looked at each other with concerned looks on their faces. I buried my face back into Rob's chest. He held his arms tight around me and kissed me on the head.

"It's okay to be scared. It's a scary thing. For sixteen long years Jason has been a very important person in your life. Now, you have to live without him. But remember, you have Rebecca, Matt and I to help you through it."

"I know that, and I love all of you to death, but..."

"It's not quite the same." Matt finished.

I nodded.

"Well that's completely understandable. You and Jason had a very special relationship. One that most people can only dream about. The two of you were so close." said Rob.

"Yeah." I said.

Matt looked at me closer. "Gracie, you look exhausted and Rebecca told us you weren't getting much sleep."

I shook my head. "Nope, because every time I do, all I see is Jason suffering again. Why can't I see Jason, Rebecca, and I happy together instead? Maybe if I did, I would've tried a little harder to sleep."

None of us said anything for a long time after that. Being in Rob's arms made me feel almost as safe as when I was in Jason's and finally I was able to pull myself together some. When I sat up, Rob and Matt started to laugh a little.

"What?"

Matt pulled out a pocket mirror and put it in front of my face. I couldn't help but smile too.

"I really should get some waterproof mascara." I chuckled.

"Here." Matt licked a Kleenex and gently wiped it off. "There good as new."

"Thanks."

"You ready to go back inside?" asked Rob.

"Yeah, I think so. I need to help Rebecca."

When we got inside, the line still didn't seem any shorter. I could tell that Rebecca was trying as hard as she could to keep herself together.

"Hey, Gracie." She reached out and gave me a hug and we held tightly to each other. "You okay?"

"I'm getting a little better, I guess. You?"

"Hanging in there as best I can. Gracie, we'll get through this. We just have to stick together, okay."

"Okay." I agreed.

"And Gracie, if you don't want to do the song you don't have to. I was wrong to pressure you into it."

"No, I'll still do it, as long as you'll still stand there next to me."

"No problem."

A half an hour later the service started. Although I tried as hard as I could to hold back the tears I couldn't any longer when Father Matthew read the Gospel reading. It was from the Gospel according to Luke 23:33-43.

When they came to the place called the Skull, they crucified him and the criminals there, one on his right, the other on his left. [Then Jesus said, "Father, forgive them, they know not what they do."] They divided his garments by casting lots. The people stood by and watched; the rulers, meanwhile, sneered at him and said, "he saved others, let him save himself if he is the chosen one, the Messiah of God." Even the soldiers jeered at him. As they approached to offer him wine they called out, "If you are King of the Jews, save yourself." Above him there was an inscription that read, "This is the King of the Jews."

Now one of the criminals hanging there reviled Jesus, saying, "Are you not the Messiah? Save yourself and us." The other, however, rebuking him, said in reply, "Have you no fear of God, for you are subject to the same condemnation? And indeed, we have been condemned justly, for the sentence we received corresponds to our crimes, but this man has done nothing criminal."

Then he said, "Jesus, remember me when you come into your kingdom."

He replied to him, "Amen, I say to you, today you will be with me in Paradise."

"The Gospel of the Lord."

"Praise to you, Lord Jesus Christ."

Father Matthew stepped out into the middle of the altar in front of the congregation. "Today, you will be with me in paradise.' That's what Jesus said to him and today, that's where Jason is now, with our Savior in Paradise looking down on all of us. Now Jason's wife, Rebecca, would like to say a few words. Rebecca?"

"Thank you for coming everyone. I know how much you all loved Jason and I can assure you that he loved all of you, too. That's the kind of person Jason was. He was a loving husband, and a great friend to all. Well, you all know, Gracie,"

I looked up and locked eyes with Rebecca and in my head I thought, 'what is she going to say?' "and to her he wasn't only a friend but also a father." I couldn't help but start crying because what she said was completely true. "Gracie's parents died when she was just four years old and by having Jason there, she never really felt like she lacked a father." I had to try and pull myself together because in a minute she'd be calling me up to do the song.

"Last night I woke up about midnight or so and Gracie was out sitting by our Christmas tree. She was working on a song in honor of Jason and although she was unwilling to at first, she agreed to sing it for all of you today. Gracie, would you come up here please?"

When I came up she gave me a hug. She wiped my tears and I wiped hers.

"Bare with me because I'll probably start crying." I told everyone.

Rebecca rubbed my back. "It's okay if you do." she whispered.

I took a deep breath and began to sing.

For sixteen long years
We shared in the laughter, the joy, and the tears.
Not only a friend, but the father I never had
The one person I ever wanted to call, dad
But then….

God saw him getting tired
A cure not meant to be
So he wrapped his arms around him
And whispered, "Come with me."

Now he's up in heaven
Watching from above
Gazing upon his children
And his one and only love.

You can almost hear him saying
"Don't worry about me,
My soul was lifted up to him
When God whispered, 'Come with me.'"

He taught me to do the right things
He taught me to dance, he taught me to sing
He protected me from the world
He called me his angel and his baby girl
He made me feel safe and let me know he was there
And now he's the wind that blows through my hair
Because.......

God saw him getting tired
A cure not meant to be
So he wrapped his arms around him
And whispered, "Come with me."

Now he's up in heaven
Watching from above
Gazing upon his children
And his one and only love.
You can almost hear him saying
"Don't worry about me,
My soul was lifted up to him
When God whispered, 'Come with me.'"

Our last night together he kissed my head
And I cried seeing him lie in that bed.
There's one more thing I want you to promise me
And I knew what that one thing would be

"Promise me you'll keep dancing" he said
But with tears in my eyes, I just shook my head

God saw him getting tired
A cure not meant to be
So he wrapped his arms around him
And whispered, "Come with me."

Now he's up in heaven
Watching from above
Gazing upon his children
And his one and only love.
You can almost hear him saying
"Don't worry about me,
My soul was lifted up to him
When God whispered, 'Come with me.'"

With eyes so soft and gentle he stared up at me
"Give me a kiss and go get some sleep."
I kissed him on the head.
"I love you" were the last words that I said.
"And I love you, my one and only angel."
Was his reply

I shivered as I thought about that night and my voice got shaky and
I got all choked up. I was ready to break down in tears and that's when
Rebecca took my hand. I looked back and she nodded and we both cried
as I sang:

God saw him getting tired
A cure not meant to be

So he wrapped his arms around him
And whispered, "Come with me."

Now he's up in heaven
Watching from above
Gazing upon his children
And his one and only love.
You can almost hear him saying
"Don't worry about me,
My soul was lifted up to him
When God whispered, 'Come with me.'"
When God whispered, 'Come with me.'"

I immediately reached for Rebecca. The whole church was silent and when I looked out, there wasn't a dry eye in the house. That goes for Rebecca and I, too. Neither of us could hold it back any more. I held her tight and whispered, "Jason."

Suddenly, every one started to clap and I cried even harder. I held tight to Rebecca's hand and we sat back down. I went through the rest of the of the funeral in tears. I didn't care about holding them back anymore.

After it was over everyone headed downstairs for a little reception, but I stayed behind. I took a deep breath and headed for the casket. With one look I began crying harder than ever because this person lying before me wasn't Jason. I still couldn't get over how he'd changed. I knelt down and put my hands over his.

"Jason!" I sobbed. "I don't want to say goodbye but I'll regret it if I don't. You were not only my best friend but, my father, and I love you very, very much. I don't think I told you that enough and I wish I had."

Rebecca came back upstairs and Father Matthews met her. "Rebecca, we need to close the casket so we can get it ready to go out to the cemetery for burial."

"No! Leave Gracie be. She needs this time with him. Don't rush her. Just, leave her alone and wait until she's ready." she demanded.

"Okay." he said.

I took a deep breath and pulled a piece of paper out of my pocket. "Here, this is for you. It's the song I wrote for you. You should take it up to heaven with you." I laid the song in his hand and gave him one last kiss on the cheek. His skin was ice cold. "I love you and I'll miss you always."

When I turned around, Rebecca was standing there and she was crying. "You heard the whole thing?"

"Yeah, I did." she smiled. "Gracie, the song was absolutely beautiful but I'm curious where it came from. You didn't have all that last night. Explain." she demanded.

"Well, after you went to bed, I thought about all my favorite times with Jason and everything just clicked. This morning I wrote the rest of it."

"Well, all I can say is I was wrong."

"What do you mean?"

"Last night it wasn't perfect. Now it's perfect. I know I said it before, but I'm going to say it again. Jason would be so proud of you and so am I."

"Thanks, Rebecca."

After the burial, we headed back to the house where we had a get together with just the closest friends and family. It was a good time because Rebecca, Rob, and Matt were all there. I did have to leave for a minute though because I didn't want to lose it in front of all those people. Rebecca and I talked and I was soon back to the gathering. We all thought the hardest part was over but apparently not.

CHAPTER *10*

Back to School

A few more days past and Rebecca and I spent them together. Even though it would be hard, we both knew it was time for me to return to school. I had already missed a week and a half.

"Gracie, it'll be hard, but remember that I'm just a phone call away if you need me and so are Rob and Matt."

"I know and that's the only reason I'm willing to go back because I know that I can call you if I need you." I said. "Hey, Rebecca, how should I explain it? You know I never told anyone about this part of my life because people would only pretend to be friends with me to get to you and Jason and everyone else."

"Are you sure you still want to keep that a secret?"

"I don't know. I just always thought it was the best thing to do. I guess I could come clean with the truth."

"That's up to you. Jason and I wanted you to keep it a secret when you were younger but, you didn't have to continue to as you got older because we knew you could handle it better. If you don't want to keep it a secret, you don't have to."

"I don't know if I want to or not."

"Well, whatever you choose, I'll be behind you."

"Thanks."

~~ ~~ ~~ ~~ ~~ ~~ ~~ ~~ ~~ ~~

When I got home, Melissa was waiting on the porch. I knew she probably would be. She was unable to come to the funeral because she couldn't get off work. "Gracie." she reached out and gave me a hug and wouldn't let go. "Are you doing okay?"

"I'm doing as good as I can be, but I'm doing even better when I'm not talking about it."

"Sorry."

"It's fine. Let's just go inside, okay. It's cold out here."

She made my favorite dinner, tacos, and we just talked most of the night. I went to bed at 11, but no matter how hard I tried I still couldn't sleep. I'd still wake up screaming within a half an hour. All I could think was, how am ever I going to get through this?

I was up early the next morning which was fine because I had school anyway. I had to be at school by seven for select choir which gave me three hours to pull myself together.

~~ ~~ ~~ ~~ ~~ ~~ ~~ ~~ ~~ ~~

When I walked into select choir, Miss Wilson was sitting at her desk. Miss Wilson is our director and one of the few people at school that knew about me and Jason. I was the first one in the room which was good because she also knew that I never told anyone. When I opened the door she looked up.

"Gracie." her face and voice were full of concern.

"Hi." I fought back the tears as she reached out to me and gave me a hug. It helped. Miss Wilson is another person I can always go to and who'll always be there for me. She's one of the few people I would go to when I couldn't have Jason.

"I'm so sorry, Gracie. Are you doing okay?" When she began rubbing my back I lost it. The tears began to flow again and I just felt so exhausted.

"Not really." I finally said. "I don't have much of an appetite and I've barely slept since he died."

She eyed me carefully. "You have lost a lot of weight and you have circles under your eyes."

"I know."

"Don't let it get to the point of hospitalization again." she said with concern. She was also one of the few that knew the reason for it before.

"That's what Rebecca said, but trust me, I'm not trying to nor did I mean for it to happen the first time. The reason I'm not sleeping is because every time I fall asleep, I see Jason suffering again and I wake up screaming. I just can never go back to sleep afterwards."

She was about to say something else but the rest of the choir members came piling in the room like a pack of wolves, so she refrained. She knew I didn't want them to know about it.

"Gracie!" they all said with excitement. "Where've you been?"

Although Rebecca and I talked about it, I still couldn't bring myself to tell them the truth. So I just said, "I've been sick."

"Oh, well we're glad you're feeling better."

"Thanks." I said as cheerfully as I could, trying to break a smile. I looked over at Miss Wilson who was watching me with concern. I wasn't feeling better. I felt terrible. I missed Jason, I was so tired that I couldn't stand it, and I felt weak in the knees.

Some of the teachers knew about me and Jason and some didn't. I stuck to the sick story for those that didn't. The ones who knew the truth were Coach Roberts because Rebecca told him that day, Mrs. Johnson, the Biology teacher, because she's married to my cousin, and of course Miss Wilson and they all knew that they weren't to say anything about it.

During third period Mrs. Smith, the school principal, came over the intercom and said, "Don't forget, tomorrow is our school trip to see the Nutcracker Ballet at the Mountain Music Theatre. Everyone **must** attend. So please be sure to bring a sack lunch or you will be going without one for the entire day. Thank you."

All the life went out of my face and I wanted to scream. 'I can't watch that ballet. I just can't!' I thought.

I held back the tears until I got to fourth period and I let it loose. It was okay, though, because I had choir fourth period (a separate class from select) and Miss Wilson was the director there too. She would understand. I was in a blind rage when I walked into the door and as soon as she saw my face hers turned serious and her eyes were concerned.

"Gracie, what happened?"

"I can't go to that tomorrow, I CAN'T." My rage turned into fear and that came through in my voice and face.

"You mean the ballet?"

"Yes, the ballet. Mrs. Smith said we **all** have to go. I'm not ready for that. I just lost Jason."

"I agree. You're not ready for that. Don't worry, I'll fix it. Do I have permission to let her in on the secret?"

I nodded.

"I'll be right back then."

"Okay." I sat there in silence while I waited. I was there alone because everyone in that hour was out sick. I wished I could call Rebecca. I knew that she'd be against it, too. It was hard waiting but, within ten minutes, Miss Wilson was back. She looked a little peeved. I knew that could only mean one thing and she quickly confirmed it.

"She won't budge. She said **EVERYONE** is going. No one is getting out of it under any circumstances."

I grabbed the necklace and held it tight. "Miss Wilson, since no one else is here, would it be alright if I....?"

"Called Rebecca." she finished.

I nodded in confirmation.

"Yeah, go ahead. Put it on speaker phone though because I want to talk to her too."

"Okay." I tried the house first but there was no answer. So, I dialed her cell next. It only took a couple of rings (though it seemed like a hundred) before she answered the phone.

"Hello." she answered.

"Rebecca, it's Gracie." I replied. My voice was a little shaky.

She noticed immediately because her voice immediately shifted from calm to panic. "Gracie, honey, what happened? Are you okay?" she asked.

"No!" I nearly screamed.

"Why? What's going on? Talk to me."

I sobbed. "They're making me go."

"Honey, go where and who's making you go?"

I looked at Miss Wilson and she quickly got my drift.

"Hey Rebecca, it's Lauren Wilson."

"Hi Lauren. What's going on? What is Gracie talking about?"

"What she means is that tomorrow the entire school is going on a field trip to see the Nutcracker Ballet and the principal won't let anyone out of going under any circumstances. Even after I told her why, she wouldn't give in and recognize the severity of the situation."

After she said that it was completely silent.

"Rebecca? Are you there?" I said.

"She's NOT going! She's not ready for that. Jason just died." Rebecca finally said.

"I know and I totally agree with you. However, I can't do anything about it. I can't go against the principal without losing my job." replied Miss Wilson.

"I know and I would never ask you to do that. Gracie, do you want to go?" asked Rebecca already knowing the answer.

"NO!"

"Okay, its okay. I'm just making sure. Lauren, let me talk to the principal. I'll try to straighten it out because she is not going. I won't allow it."

"Alright. Gracie why don't you come too." Miss Wilson said.

"No." said Rebecca. "I don't want her to hear what I'm going to say because right now I am furious." Miss Wilson and I looked at each other as if saying 'What exactly is she going to say?'

So, once again I was by myself. However, it didn't take long for Miss Wilson to come back down and she had the phone off of speaker but I could hear what Rebecca was saying. "Let me talk to Gracie."

I took the phone and said, "Rebecca, what did she say?"

"It's no use, Gracie. She won't listen me, Miss Wilson, or Coach Roberts."

My heart sank. I CAN'T go is all that ran through my head. I put the phone back on speaker.

"Would it be better if I stayed with her?" suggested Miss Wilson.

"That will make me feel a little better." replied Rebecca. "Gracie?" she asked.

Miss Wilson looked at me. I nodded in agreement. "Yeah, that'd be good. It'll make me feel a little better too."

"Okay."

"Lauren, take it off of speaker for a minute." said Rebecca.

"Alright."

Neither of them knew it, but I could hear everything Rebecca was saying loud and clear.

"Lauren, you need to really watch her, okay."

"I will."

"She's on her way to getting sick again and by going to this show I'm afraid it'll do her in."

"So am I and we can't let that happen."

"No we can't, but considering the fact that the Nutcracker Ballet was the first time she ever saw Jason dance it'll probably make it worse. I can see her watching the Prince and seeing only Jason up there."

"Oh yeah. I didn't think about her doing that."

'I did.' I thought. It's all I thought about ever since Mrs. Smith said that we were going.

"Watch her. Keep her safe."

"I will, I promise. Do you want to talk to Gracie."

"Yeah."

"Here you go, Gracie."

"Thanks." I said as she handed me the phone.

"Gracie, remember, if you need anything, call. I'll always be here."

"That's what Jason said!"

"Yeah, just what Jason said and please try to get some sleep tonight, okay. You need the rest more than anything."

"I promise you I do try!"

"Okay, okay. I'm sorry."

"Forget it. I don't want to fight about it anymore."

"Neither do I."

"I love you, Rebecca."

"I love you, too." she replied with a gentle voice. "I'd better let you go. The bells going to ring soon isn't it?"

"Yeah, I'll talk to you later." I hung up the phone and stood there quietly.

"Gracie, you okay?" asked Miss Wilson.

"I have to be don't I. It's the only way I'm going to get through it."

"Gracie, I'll be right there, okay. You won't be alone. I won't leave you."

That afternoon when I got home I was surprised because Aunt Melissa's car was in the driveway. She usually didn't get home until about five o'clock.

"Hey, what are you doing home so early?"

"I skipped my lunch, so I could be home when you got here. I knew today was going to be hard for you."

"You have no idea."

"Tell me all about it." When I told her about going to see the Nutcracker, she agreed with Rebecca, Miss Wilson and I. "You're not ready for that."

"Trust me, I know I'm not. Miss Wilson knows it and Rebecca knows it. We're not the ones you need to convince. Mrs. Smith is. She's the one who's making me go but she won't budge."

Melissa was almost as furious as Rebecca. She called Mrs. Smith here and there and although she didn't yell you could tell that she was angry. However, nothing she said worked either. It was no use, she wasn't going to give in to anything we told her. I realized that all there was left to do was pray to God and to Jason for strength.

"Please Lord, help me get through this. The funeral was hard enough. This is going to be just as hard if not harder. I'm not ready for it. Jason, be there with me. I need you tomorrow, PLEASE!"

I tried to sleep but I couldn't. The thought of what tomorrow would bring was too heavy on my mind and heart. I kept asking myself the same questions over and over.

"What's the big deal if I didn't go? Why is Mrs. Smith being so thoughtless? Why won't she listen to Coach Roberts, Miss Wilson, Rebecca, Melissa or me? What is her problem with it all? Seriously, what is so terrible about me not going?"

I was torturing myself with these questions and I knew I shouldn't be but I just couldn't let it go.

CHAPTER 11

The Ballet

We left school at 9 a.m. the next morning.

"Gracie, why don't you ride with me?" said Miss Wilson.

I nodded in complete agreement. I wanted to ride with her anyway because one, she knew how I was feeling and, two, I really didn't want to be on a bus where it was going to be chaotic and noisy. I wasn't in the mood to be in that kind of atmosphere.

"Did you get any sleep last night, Gracie?" was the first thing that she asked me.

I shook my head. "No."

She sighed. "Gracie."

"I know, I know. I don't particularly like it either." I stared out the window and watched all the cars and trees go by. I touched my chest and I panicked. "Oh no!"

"Gracie, what's the matter?"

"Jason's cross. I don't have it on. Now I really can't do this." I tried to calm myself down but I couldn't.

"It'll be okay. I'm still here."

"I know, but.." I didn't finish what I was saying because my cell phone started ringing. "Hello."

"Gracie, it's me."

"Oh, Melissa."

"Gracie, I found your cross on the floor. Did you mean to leave it?"

"No, it must of fell off on my way out."

"Well, I'll meet you at the theater and bring it to you."

"Really? Oh my gosh, thank you."

"No problem, Hun. I love you."

"Love you, too."

"Everything ok?" asked Miss Wilson as I hung up the phone.

"Yeah. The necklace fell off on my way out. She's bringing it to the theater which I'll be forever grateful to her for doing."

"Good." she said with relief. "Hey Gracie, Rebecca was telling me about the song you wrote for Jason yesterday. She said there wasn't a dry eye in the church."

"No, there wasn't."

"Will you sing it for me?"

I hesitated a little but I eventually said, "I guess I can." As I sang the song I felt my pulse racing and my heart felt as if it was going a hundred miles an hour. I couldn't finish. I couldn't even get through the second verse before breaking down in tears. I started hyperventilating and I couldn't catch my breath. Why couldn't I get through it?

"Gracie, I'm sorry, I'm sorry." She pulled over into a grocery store parking lot. "Deep breaths. It's okay. I'm sorry for asking you to do it."

"It's not your fault. You didn't do anything wrong." I said struggling to get just one breath. This had never happened before and it scared me more than anything else ever did. This was a time when Jason would be the only one who could make it better (of course if he were here, then this wouldn't be happening). Just that thought alone got me crying again but I didn't let Miss Wilson see. "Come on. Let's just go. If we don't, we'll be late. Then we will get into trouble. Mrs. Smith is already angry. Although not as angry as we are, but let's just go. I don't want to cause anymore trouble."

"Are you sure you're okay?"

"Yes. I just want to get this over with." I said with determination.

"Alright." she replied with a little hesitation.

I was slowly getting back my breath and when we pulled in front of the theater I quickly wiped my eyes. Aunt Melissa was a few parking spaces away and I still wasn't quite breathing steadily. When Melissa realized it, her face turned serious. "You okay?"

"Yeah." I lied.

"Okay. Here." She put the necklace around my neck and I immediately found it easier to breathe within seconds, which puzzled me a little.

"Thank you."

"It was no problem Gracie. You know I only work a few blocks down."

"Yeah, but still."

"Come on Gracie!" I heard Kelly yell.

"I'm coming! I'll see you later, Melissa."

"Bye, Hun!" She blew me a kiss as I ran to catch up with the others and Miss Wilson held out her hand and I took hold of it.

The wait in line was long. We were forty-five minutes early, too. There must've been a lot of schools coming to see the ballet because the place was packed full of teenagers, teachers, and chaperones. I stayed close to Miss Wilson so I could be sure I sat next to her.

Being in all the crowds made me dizzy again. I never had much experience being in a large crowd of people I didn't know and I wasn't quite sure how to handle it. Although Jason was a celebrity, when we were together he was careful to avoid all the paparazzi so it could just be him, me and Rebecca with no interruptions. Every once in a while a fan or two would come up and that was okay but when a big crowd would come he would very politely shoo them away. He never wanted me to have to deal with that kind of stuff. I always liked that he did it but right now I was kind of wishing he wouldn't have because maybe I'd be doing a little better than I was at the moment.

It took us about twenty minutes to get through the line. When we walked into the theater, it took my breath away. It was absolutely gorgeous. There were columns and it seemed like it was a mile long. There were balconies all around and the stage was made of pure, stained wood. The seats were comfortable too. They had a red velvet cover on the seat and back of the chairs and ours were just about dead center.

Miss Wilson and I took an aisle seat and Coach Roberts sat a couple rows behind just in case. When the ballet first started it wasn't too bad, however, the prince hadn't come out yet.

As it got closer and closer though, my body began to tense up and I felt my blood run cold. When he did come out, what Rebecca and I had feared the most happened. When the Prince came out I didn't see the guy who was playing him, all I saw was Jason as I did what seemed eight long years ago. I broke out into a cold sweat and I cried as I heard Jason's voice.

"Just relax and look into my eyes……It's okay, Jason's here, you're safe….Gracie!…..oh, my sweet angel."

I gripped the arm rests so tight that my knuckles turned white. I felt my body temperature rise and my whole body felt weak. "Miss Wilson." I sobbed. "Help!" I tried not to scream so nobody would notice.

She immediately looked back at Coach. He came up and knelt down beside me. "Gracie."

"I can't do this anymore. All I'm seeing is Jason. Get me out of here. PLEASE!" I tried to stand up but my legs were too wobbly and weak. I fell forward into Coach's arms and he cradled me.

"It's okay, I'm here, you're safe."

I began crying and shaking uncontrollably. Why did he have to say that?

"Coach." said Miss Wilson.

"What?"

"You can't say that to her. Jason always said that to her."

His face panicked and he looked guilty. "Wait a minute. That would mean that…"

"Yeah, you probably just made it worse."

"Oh no!" He rushed me out of the theater and my vision became blurry. I couldn't focus anymore. There was only one thing that was clear when we got out of the theater and I screamed out her name.

"Rebecca!"

"I'm here." She felt my head. "You're burning up." She sighed in anger. "I knew this was going to happen and I promised Jason that I wouldn't let it."

"It's not your fault." Miss Wilson reassured her. "If anyone's to blame it's Mrs. Smith. She's the one that made her go even though we all told her no. She's the only one that should be feeling guilty right now."

Then Rebecca said something that made me very curious but I didn't ask her about it. I didn't feel good enough to. I had a major headache, I was completely exhausted, and I was shaking so bad that it felt like I was in an earthquake.

"That's it. The time is now. When she wakes up." she said.

"The time for what?" asked Miss Wilson who was almost as curious as I was.

"Once she's feeling good enough it'll be time to give her the letter." That's the last thing I remember before drifting off to sleep.

CHAPTER 12

The Letter

I woke up in a hospital bed coming out of a deep, deep sleep. It took a minute for things to focus. When they finally did, I gasped in shock and my eyes were wide. All around the room were get well soon balloons, flowers (from carnations to roses, and daisies to tulips) and next to me was a soft, pink teddy bear with a note next to it.

Dear Gracie,

Hope you get well soon. I love you very much.

Rob

I couldn't figure out how long I'd been asleep. I figured it wasn't long because I still felt completely exhausted. My body still felt warm and I had an oxygen tube up my nose to help me breathe. They must of pumped me full of antibiotics and medication because I felt really groggy.

Where was Rebecca? I tried to stand up but I was light-headed so I sat back down. I was in a hospital gown anyway. I hate the fact that they don't close. My jeans and t-shirt were on the nightstand next to my bed. I quickly put them on and grabbed hold of the monitor before trying to stand up again.

I was wobbly at first but I quickly found my balance. I needed to find

Rebecca. I had to know what was going on. I couldn't remember anything that happened. Why was I here?

I slowly made my way out the door. "Rebecca!" I was surprised at how weak and soft sounding my voice was. I tried to walk faster but that made for a major headache like when you eat too much ice cream at once and you get a brain freeze. "Rebecca!" I called again. I looked around. I saw no one that I knew. So, I called a different name. The one name that always came when I called. "Jason!"

"Gracie! What are you doing up?" said Rebecca with a panic.

"Rebecca, what do you mean 'what am I doing up?' Where's Jason?"

"What?!" she said in disbelief. She turned around quickly. "Rob!" she screamed.

"Rebecca what's…." he started. "Oh no, Gracie." He immediately cradled me in his arms and carried me back to the room.

"Rob, she wanted to know where Jason was? She isn't remembering and it's scaring me. She didn't know why she was here either. I'm going to get the doctor." she said.

"Go, go! I'll get her back to the room." He gently laid me in the bed and covered me up with the blankets. "Here we go."

"Rob, where's Jason?!"

His face went blank as if he didn't know what to say. "Gracie, he's gone." he said gently but also with a little desperation.

I began to shake. I began to sweat too. The door opened and Rebecca and the Doctor came in. Rebecca's face was concerned and scared.

"Why is she asking where Jason is? Why doesn't she know why she's here? Why isn't she remembering anything?"

The doctor took my temperature and his eyes went wide as he read the temperature. "Her temperature spiked way up again to 103.1"

"Oh, God."

"Well, that is too high, but there is some good in that. That means the high fever is causing the hallucinations and the loss of memory. Once the fever goes down, she won't remember any of this and she'll remember the fact that Jason is gone." The doctor then put a cold towel on my forehead and left.

"Rob, I promised Jason that I wouldn't let this happen again. Not only did it happen again, but this time it's worse. Much worse."

"What do you mean?" asked Rob.

"Last time she was just a little overwhelmed and the fever only got to 100.1. Plus, they were able to bring it down quickly and keep it down. This time she wasn't just overwhelmed. She wasn't getting any sleep, she wasn't eating, she was losing weight, and now her fever's back up. Why is it so much worse?"

Rob shrugged his shoulders but then almost immediately snapped his fingers and with confidence said, "I think I know why."

"What?" Rebecca asked with a little disbelief.

"Think about it. The first time, it was a shock and, yes, it was a little overwhelming, but remember he was still here. She hadn't lost him yet. She just knew that she was going to. This time she did lose him. He wasn't there anymore when she needed him and that was scary to her because there was never a time when he wasn't there. Last time he was at least still there."

"Rebecca." I managed to say.

She shifted around and looked at me square on. "Gracie, honey, what is it?"

"I'm cold."

She smiled and wrapped the cover tighter around me. "There you go. Now close your eyes and get some sleep." She kissed me on the forehead. "She's burning up." She looked at Rob, her eyes welling up with tears.

"She'll be okay. I promise. Jason will watch over her. She'll be alright." he reassured her.

꒛꒛ ꒛꒛ ꒛꒛ ꒛꒛ ꒛꒛ ꒛꒛ ꒛꒛ ꒛꒛ ꒛꒛ ꒛꒛

When I woke up I knew it was morning (although I had no clue what day) because the sun was just rising over the clouds. Rebecca was asleep and Rob was looking out the window and he looked deep in thought.

"Rob." I said quietly.

He raced to my side and felt my forehead. "Rebecca," he said with relief "her fever's broke."

Rebecca jumped up out of the chair and raised her hands. "Oh, thank God." It was nice seeing Rebecca smile. It was contagious. Everyone smiled when she smiled.

"I'll go tell the others." said Rob.

"Others?" I asked.

"Yeah." Rebecca replied. "Matt, Melissa, Miss Wilson, and Melanie (Mrs. Johnson who of course I only call that at school since she's now my cousin) are all out in the waiting room."

"Rebecca, how long have I been asleep?"

"A couple days."

"Oh my gosh!"

"Don't worry about it. You needed the rest."

I sighed in relief. "Well, I guess that means I never saw Jason suffering."

"It doesn't quite mean that. You did wake up screaming 'JASON!' a number of times."

"I don't remember that."

"Your fever was so high that you most likely won't. You probably don't remember getting out of bed, or asking why you were here, or even asking where Jason was."

"No, I don't and I hate it when I can't remember things."

"Don't worry! None of it's important."

Then Rob came into the room. "Rebecca, could you come out here for a second?" he asked.

"Sure. I'll be right back."

Soon I heard talking. She was talking to a woman out in the hall.

Rebecca's voice was agitated. I couldn't figure out exactly who the other woman was. I looked at Rob and whispered, "Who is it?"

"I don't know. I don't recognize her." he answered also in a whisper.

"Gracie, someone wants to talk to you." said Rebecca poking her head into the room.

"Who?" I asked. The woman walked in and I had to literally hold my jaw so it wouldn't drop. "Mrs. Smith?" I said in disbelief.

"Hello Gracie. I wanted to say I'm sorry about everything. I was wrong to make you go and I should've listened to all of you."

"I forgive you. However, I do have a few of questions that have haunted me and I would appreciate some answers."

"Okay. What's that?"

"Why was it such a big deal that I go? What was so important about it that EVERYONE had to go? Why didn't you listen to all of us when we tried to tell you why I couldn't go?"

"I thought…" she hesitated. "I thought it was all a lie and just an excuse to get out of going because most teenagers think ballet is boring. I had so many excuses from so many students that I wasn't going to let ANYONE out of it."

"Okay. First of all, I AM a ballet dancer along with many other types of dance. Two, are you saying that you didn't believe I knew Jason Baylor?"

"Yes." she shamefully replied.

"Rebecca and Melissa talked to you. And by the way, Miss Wilson and Coach Roberts also talked to you. That means that you didn't even believe your own teachers. What made you suddenly believe it anyway?" I tried to be respectful but I was so pissed at this woman.

"When I met Rebecca, Rob, and Matt."

"So, basically as soon as you saw the celebrities?"

"Yes." Her face showed shame and so did her voice.

"You know to me they aren't just celebrities. They are my family and

Rebecca and Jason are like my mother and father." With that Rebecca looked up and she seemed surprised.

"I'm so sorry. I truly am. It was wrong of me. Everything you said was true and I hope you can all forgive me."

"I do. I truly do." I said with one hundred percent sincerity.

"Thank you." She mustered up a smile and then quietly left.

Rebecca looked at Rob. "Could you excuse us for a minute? I need to talk to Gracie alone if you know what I mean."

Rob nodded. "I gotcha. I'll be outside."

I looked at Rebecca very curiously. What were they talking about?

"I'm not in trouble am I?" I asked just joking around.

She laughed. "No don't worry. You're not in trouble. Gracie, I have something for you."

"What is it?"

"It's a letter and a DVD. They're from Jason."

"What?" I asked in surprise.

"He gave it to me the night before he died, while you were out on Lightning. He had a letter for me and a letter for you, as well as a DVD he made. He instructed me not to read mine until after the funeral and to give you yours when I felt the time was right."

"How'd you know the right time was now? There were so many times before that would've been good."

"You're right. There were many times that I thought it was. But, when I was about to say something it's like I could hear Jason telling me 'not now.' However, when I saw Coach Roberts carry you out, in my heart I heard him say, 'the time is when she wakes up.'" With that, she reached into her purse and pulled out a DVD and an envelope. "Here."

I took a deep breath and quickly opened up the letter. I was anxious to find out what he had said. I took a deep breath and as I read the words the tears freely flowed down my face. It read:

Katie Peterson

Dear Gracie,

There are so many things that I never told you enough. Let me start with this. I love you very, very much and no one could be any prouder of you than I am in the person you have become.

I can't begin to describe what a joy it was to watch you grow up. I will forever be in God's debt for allowing me to be there when you took your first step, said your first word, started discovering the world, comfort you during your first broken heart, and watch you blossom into a young woman.

You were always the daughter I never had and that makes me think of your father and how sad it makes me that he didn't get the chance to watch you grow. I miss him and your mother so much. It's so unfair and cruel that both Rebecca and I got to spend so much time with your parents and you so little. I want you to know, when your parents died, Rebecca and I wanted to do everything we could to make sure you didn't feel an emptiness because they were no longer here, but also know that we knew we could never ever fully replace them.

Nobody ever could. Your parents were the most compassionate, generous, honorable, and loving people I have ever had the pleasure to know and you are exactly like them.

I never told you this, but you didn't get your talent for dancing from me. You got it from your mother. Like you, she had a passion for it and I want you to continue to dance. With that being said, I know you told me that you couldn't dance without me, but every time you put that cross around your neck, I am right there and I believe you can do anything that you set your mind to.

*Remember that I will **NEVER** fully leave you. I am watching you always and still protecting you and wishing only the best for you. Also, if you ever need me pop in this DVD. It's full of our dances, pictures, and videos so you'll never forget. And one more thing, remember that you always have been and forever will be my one and only angel.*

Love you always,

Jason

With tears running down my cheeks I grasped Jason's cross and whispered, "I love you too Jason!"

Rebecca sat down on the bed next to me and threw her arms around me. "It's okay."

"You know Rebecca when I said to Mrs. Smith that you and Jason are like my mother and father, I meant it. But, you seemed surprised. Why?"

"Oh, I don't know."

"I do. When I was kneeling at the casket I said I never told him enough that he was like my father. Well, I realized that I especially never told you enough. You are like my mother. You are the mother I never got to have and always wanted."

"Oh, honey. You didn't have to say anything to either of us. We already knew it because the love you showed us everyday said it all."

As she kissed me on the forehead there was a knock at the door. "Come in." I called still a little emotional.

"Everything okay?" asked Rob.

"Yeah."

"Could you stand a few visitors than?"

"Of course. Who?"

"Hey Gracie!" It was Matt, Miss Wilson, Melanie, and Aunt Melissa.

"Hi everybody!" Matt was the first one that I reached out for. Out of all six people in the room (not including myself) he was the only one who really knew Jason as well as I did, who I hadn't gotten to see yet.

It was nice having the people I loved there with me. However, the doctor said they had to leave after only 15 minutes because I needed the rest. It was okay though, everyone except Rebecca had to leave for work anyway.

Once everyone was gone, the doctor took my temperature again. This time it was a safe 98.6 so it was back to normal. However, they still wanted me to stay a couple more nights because I still didn't have much strength.

At noon, Rebecca left for a little while and got us some cheeseburgers. She said I needed to eat and there was no way I was going to eat hospital food. I slept most of the time that she was gone, but no matter how much I slept, I still felt completely burned out.

When she got back I asked, "Do you have your laptop with you?"

She smiled. "You want to watch the DVD?"

I nodded.

"Alright." We got out the food and I made room on the bed. When I popped in the DVD, I was amazed. Jason had made it look like a real movie menu and there was a picture of us dancing in the background. He titled it 'Me and My Angel.' It was all separated into dances, pictures and other videos that ranged from birthdays to Christmas', from my first summer in L.A. at the age of 4 (right after my parents passed away) to my eighth grade graduation.

Rebecca and I watched the entire thing. We ate, watched, and cried the whole time. What I loved the most though was that he recorded himself singing the song that he wrote for me and put it with the slide show of pictures. Now I could hear him sing that song anytime. He also put two of our favorite songs (there were lots of pictures) with it. The first was the last song we ever danced to, "In My Daughters Eyes" by Martina McBride and the second was "I Hope You Dance" by LeAnn Womack.

When it was over I said, "Hey, Rebecca?"

"Yeah."

"Will you do something for me?"

"Sure."

"When I get out of here it'll almost be Christmas break. When I come down, will you help me create a dance for Christmas Eve like we always do."

"Oh, Gracie, I don't know about that."

"Having you being the one instructing me is the only way that I can do what Jason asked me to do. I have to do one last dance in his honor. I have to. Please, help me."

"What made you change your mind? Two days ago you refused to dance at all because you couldn't do it without Jason there by your side."

"This letter and DVD changed my mind. When he said 'every time you put that cross around your neck, I'm right there.' When he said that it also made me realize what happened before in the car with Miss Wilson and when I met up with Aunt Melissa."

"What are you talking about?"

"On the way to the ballet, Miss Wilson asked if I'd sing the song I wrote for Jason for her. I realized before that, that I hadn't had the cross on. It fell off on my way out. Aunt Melissa found it and called me telling me that she would bring it. In the middle of the second verse I lost it to the point of hyperventilation. When we got there I was breathing a little better but not nearly enough. However, when she put the cross around my neck my breathing was suddenly steady and normal. Now, I realize it was because Jason was there and now I know that I won't have to do it without him as long as I have on that cross."

"Well alright then. As soon as you come for break we'll get started. Be thinking of the song you want to use."

I smiled. I was way ahead of her. The song I was going to use was already in my head.

Chapter 13

Plans

I had to stay in the hospital for a few more days until I got some strength back. Rebecca was a saint the whole time. I literally had to force her to get a ***good*** night sleep.

"Rebecca, you made me leave Jason's side to get a good night sleep in my bed and that situation was a lot worse. I'll be okay, I promise. I'll see you in the morning." I had to keep telling her about a hundred times.

Finally around 10, I convinced her. "Alright. I'll see you tomorrow. I love you." I could tell that she was reluctant to leave me there alone.

"Love you, too. I'll be fine." She kissed me on the forehead and headed out the door.

At midnight, I shut off the television and snuggled under the covers and I soon drifted off to sleep. I kept on Jason's cross through the night and it ended up being the first time I slept through the night without waking up screaming his name. I did dream about Jason, but this time I didn't see him suffering again. Instead, I saw a number of things: our skiing trip when he told me about how Rebecca and I had saved his life, when he carried me after I broke my ankle and said 'it's okay, Jason's here, you're safe', my 16th birthday (my last birthday with him), and our last Christmas together when we danced and he had given me the cross. I hoped that I could dream about those things from now on.

~~ ~~ ~~ ~~ ~~ ~~ ~~ ~~ ~~ ~~

It was almost 10 o'clock before I woke up the next morning. When I did, Rebecca was there with glazed donuts, coffee, and was smiling from ear to ear.

"What are you so happy about?"

"The nurses told me that you slept all night."

"Yeah I did. I saw Jason but he wasn't suffering. Instead I saw the three of us together again. It helped a lot and it felt so real."

When she still had a huge smile on her face, I knew that she still had something more to say.

I gave her a look and she finally said. "There's more good news."

"What's that?"

"The doctor said you can come home today because your fever has stayed down and you've now slept through the night."

First I smiled, then I laughed. "Today's the last day of school before Christmas break."

Rebecca laughed too. "Gracie, he wasn't going to let you go back until after the new year anyway."

"Oh, okay. I'm glad I got my finals done early then." I said with relief.

Rebecca smiled and kind of shook her head. "Oh, by the way, you, Melissa, and I are going to have lunch about noon if you're feeling up to it."

"That sounds great actually."

"We'll leave for L.A. tomorrow." Rebecca continued.

"Okay." I always spent Christmas with Rebecca and Jason because Melissa and her boyfriend, Eric, always went to his parents house for Christmas and New Years and I never did feel totally comfortable there.

The rest of the holidays Melissa and I did spend together. The fourth of July, Melissa would come down to L.A. for a week or so.

Lunch was great. We went to Olive Garden and laughed and talked for hours. We didn't end up leaving the restaurant until 2:30 and the only reason we left then was because Melissa had to go back to work.

Rebecca and I went home and I made sure I had everything I needed for L.A. that wasn't there. When Melissa got home, the three of us watched a movie, then settled into bed.

Rebecca and I got up at the crack of dawn the next morning since we were driving back to L.A. Rebecca had gotten in the car at midnight the morning of the ballet and arrived only two hours before Coach and Miss Wilson brought me out of the theater.

In the car I got to thinking about the dance but I couldn't come up with anything. When we stopped for lunch I finally admitted it. "Rebecca, please tell me you have some kind of thoughts about this dance. Jason always came up with the moves before."

She smiled. She knew something I didn't. "Don't worry about that. It's all under control. You just think of what song you want to use."

"I already know what song I want."

"Oh, really. What?" she asked in anticipation. I leaned over and whispered it in her ear.

CHAPTER 14

Breath of Heaven

Rebecca smiled. "Gracie, that's perfect."

"When I decided to do the dance it was the first thing that came to mind."

"Well, I can tell you right now, whenever he heard that song, the only person he ever thought about was you because, like he told you on that ski trip, if it wasn't for the two of us coming into his life when we did, he would of taken his own life. You held him together."

"So did you."

"Well, it's still perfect. It was one of his favorites too."

"It's settled then. That's the song."

We were quiet for a long time and I soon drifted off to sleep. By the time I woke up we were home. My favorite place in the world.

I headed upstairs when we got inside and put all my stuff in my room. Then I took a quick shower. It felt really good because I hadn't gotten to take a shower since the night before the ballet. I meant to take one last night but I fell asleep. I was getting in my pajamas when Rebecca called me. "Gracie, could you come down here please?"

"Be there in a minute!" I replied.

When I went downstairs, she was sitting on the couch in the family room and it looked like she had a DVD in.

"What's going on?"

"Remember when I said the dance routine was all under control?"

"Yeah."

"Well here you go." she patted the couch and I sat down next to her. When she pressed play I gasped.

"Hey Gracie." It was Jason.

"What?" I was completely shocked. "Rebecca, what is this?"

She paused it and turned to me. "Look Gracie, Jason knew a long time ago that when he asked you to keep dancing you would say no and you couldn't do it without him. He thought this might help if you ever changed your mind."

"You mean this DVD is him teaching me more routines?"

"Yes, that's exactly what it is."

I smiled and turned back to the screen and Rebecca pressed play.

"Gracie, I've created a few dances for you so you don't have to quit having me as your teacher right away. Rebecca is there and she'll guide you through and help you as I teach you the steps."

My eyes were getting teary. This was exactly what I needed in order to get through this. He had all the categories covered. Ballet, Jazz, the Tango, Tap, Freestyle, Clogging, the Salsa, Ballroom, Hip-Hop, Modern, Swing, and my personal favorite Country and Western because it was both Jason's and my roots. He even had a dance created to the song I had chosen, "Breath of Heaven" by Amy Grant. It really was perfect because he was holding me together just like the song said.

> Breath of Heaven
> Hold me together
> Be forever near me
> Breath of Heaven

Jason was the Breath of Heaven. He would hold me together and when I put that cross around my neck he would be forever near me.

"Just believe in yourself just as I do. I love you." Jason concluded.

Rebecca stopped the tape and said, "So, when do you want to get started?"

"Now?!"

"How about tomorrow morning? It's getting late."

"Okay." I said a little disappointed. She just smiled.

ᴘ ᴘ ᴘ ᴘ ᴘ ᴘ ᴘ ᴘ ᴘ ᴘ ᴘ ᴘ ᴘ ᴘ ᴘ ᴘ ᴘ ᴘ ᴘ ᴘ

I was up at 6 o'clock anxious to get started. I had a protein bar, an apple, an orange and some apple juice for breakfast. I didn't eat a big one because I knew we were going to be doing some hard dancing. I put on my dance shorts and t-shirt (what I always wore when learning a new dance).

When I went down to the studio, Rebecca was already down there getting ready.

"Oh, hey. I didn't think you were up yet." I said in surprise.

"You ready to get started?"

"Yep."

"Good. Let's just watch it first so you can get an idea of what the dance will look like when it's finished."

"Okay. Before we start though, I have a question."

"Alright."

"You and Jason always did a dance together, too, on Christmas Eve."

"Yeah."

"Are you going to do a dance?"

"Not this time Gracie. Not this time."

"Why not?"

"Because, I want you to do it and really so did Jason."

"Rebecca, he would want you to do it too."

"Gracie, stop. I want you to do it. Now let's get started."

I didn't mention it again. I could tell that she'd made up her mind.

Jason started out slow and didn't worry about the music yet. He mixed a lot of the styles together but he mostly used ballet (which was the easiest to do alone). He didn't use many leaps or jumps because this was a very solemn song. However, he did throw a couple in there. Then he showed me what it all looked like with the music. It looked gorgeous and I could only hope that I could make it look that beautiful and do him proud.

Rebecca and I worked on it all morning. We only had a few days and I was bound and determined to get it right. She did convince me to stop for lunch and we took a break after so it could digest. Eating then doing heavy dance rehearsals is not a good idea. We took a couple of hours and returned to the dance floor.

The days were long and tiring but it was also fun. Each day I had to play the DVD less and less and by the last day it was flawless. That afternoon Rebecca and I went out for lunch and shopping at the mall. She wanted me to pick out a new outfit for the dance which she insisted on paying for.

I wanted to find something in red because it was Jason's favorite color and this dance was all about honoring him in every way possible. I found one that had short sleeves, a scoop neck, and sparkles. It came just above my knee and we both cried when I came out because every single aspect and detail was perfect in every way.

"Rebecca you don't have to buy it. You already paid for lunch and helped me with that dance. Plus, this dress is too expensive."

"Don't be silly. It's only $40. Besides, I want to."

"Thank you." I said with complete sincerity.

"You're welcome."

That night we relaxed. "No rehearsal tonight." Rebecca said.

We made it a complete girl's night. We made popcorn and watched our favorite Christmas movies all night long. Including Christmas Shoes, The Holiday, The Grinch with Jim Carrey, The Nativity Story, and It's a Wonderful Life. We laughed and cried. Jason loved to watch movies, especially at Christmas time.

As we finished up the last movie it finally hit me. Tomorrow is Christmas Eve. "Rebecca, do you think I can pull this off?" I asked beginning to doubt myself.

"No, I don't think you can." My face fell but then she smiled. "I know you can."

"Really?!"

"Yeah, and you want to know why?"

"Why?"

"Gracie, in four days you have learned a rather difficult dance and you do it flawlessly. When I watched you this morning you took my breath away and almost had me crying. It looked as if you'd been practicing it for weeks, rather than a few days. Jason would be extremely proud of you. I know I keep telling you that but it's the truth."

I smiled. "Thanks for everything Rebecca. I wouldn't have learned it nearly as quickly if it weren't for you helping and guiding me through it."

"Gracie, I didn't do all that much. Jason taught you the steps, not me."

"You did a great deal. Like I said without you there to help, I wouldn't have been able to pick it up and pull it off in four days. So, once again I'll say, thank you for everything. I love you…." I hesitated, "mom."

She raised her head and looked directly into my eyes. She was in shock and couldn't say anything for a long time. Then she smiled from ear to ear. "You're welcome Gracie and I love you, too very, very much. You are my daughter." She looked at her watch and said "It's getting late, Hun. What do you say we get some sleep. It's a big day tomorrow."

"Yeah, it is getting kind of late."

"Good night, Gracie." she said and kissed me on the forehead.

"Night."

I did my normal nightly routine. I put on my pajamas, brushed my teeth, and washed all the make-up off my face. The warm water woke me up, so I crawled under the covers and watched all of our Christmas Eve dances again for inspiration. Then I watched a video that I hadn't ever seen before. We must of accidentally skipped it the day we watched it at the hospital. I gasped in shock when I pressed play. It was a story that Jason always told me and one that I'd always loved to hear. It was the day he and Rebecca came and saw me at the hospital the day I was born and one of the best parts was seeing my mom and dad. I could see myself in my mom's face and my smile was like dad's.

I must have been more tired than I thought because the last thing I remember was watching the slide show of pictures with the sound of Jason singing "My Angel." I dreamed once again of Jason, Rebecca and me on our ski trip, our campouts, and just times that we enjoyed each other's company. It was a peaceful night, and like before, I hoped and prayed that I would continue to dream those dreams and see Jason happy and healthy and never see him suffering ever again.

The next morning I woke up refreshed and was ready to face what lied ahead. I was ready to do what I'd been working so hard for. I was ready to honor Jason and have his spirit run through my body and soul and inspire me to do the best dance of my life in his honor.

CHAPTER 15

One Last Dance

The first thing I did that morning was practice the dance a couple of times with the dress on. That way I could really be sure I could still easily do the dance without ripping the dress or something while I did the leaps and jumps. I sighed in relief after I was done. "Perfect." I whispered. I turned to the mirror and smiled.

Rebecca was standing in the doorway. "Don't do too much. You don't want to ware yourself out."

"I'm done! I'm done! I just wanted to try it once or twice in the dress just to be sure that it really worked.

She chuckled, then nodded. "Come on upstairs and change. Breakfast is almost ready."

We always had a traditional breakfast on Christmas Eve and Christmas morning. Rebecca was an amazing cook. When I came upstairs the aroma made my mouth water. It was my favorite. Warm waffles with butter (no syrup), a glass of ice cold milk, and a bowl of fresh fruit (grapes, honey dew, canolope, and watermelon).

After we finished cleaning up, Rebecca started making a list of things to do in order to get ready for the party.

"Anything I can do to help with the party?"

"The only thing that needs to be done is getting the food ready because the house is basically already clean. I was going to go through one more time to be sure though."

"I'll make the brownies!" I smiled. Brownies were my specialty and were my favorite because I could eat the leftover chocolate afterward.

Rebecca smiled. "I knew that's what you were going to say you'd do. Alright, you make the brownies and I'll make sure that the house is clean."

While she did some last minute dusting I got the ingredients out for the brownies. While the oven preheated, I mixed the vegetable oil, water, and eggs into a large mixing bowl like the recipe called for. I couldn't help but think how weird it was to make brownies without Jason. Both of us loved chocolate and we'd always sneak a spoon in to get extra chocolate when Rebecca wasn't looking. Once it was mixed up well enough I poured it all into a pan (leaving just enough for me to eat) and popped them in the oven. They had to cook for about 25 to 30 minutes so I asked Rebecca what else I could do.

"Gracie, why don't you just sit and relax." she insisted.

"But…." I started. "I want to help."

"Gracie, once I'm done with this room, nothing else needs to be done right now. I don't need to put out the shrimp and meat for the sandwiches until later and other than the drummies that we'll pick up this afternoon, not much else needs to be done. You know everybody brings something."

"Alright fine. I'll relax only until the brownies are done and cool. Then I'll decorate them."

"Okay, and I'll tell you what, once you're done with that we'll do something together."

I smiled from ear to ear. I loved doing things with Rebecca. We'd go horseback riding, watch movies, go shopping, go swimming, and play all kinds of board games. It's all the things I always imagined doing with my mother if she had been alive. Jason said in the letter that they wanted to try and fill the emptiness that came with losing my parents and all I could think was they truly did a great job of it. I always wanted to call Rebecca "mom" and Jason "dad" but I never had the courage to until last night when I said it to Rebecca and I never ever would have if Jason hadn't told me that. It felt good to say it.

~ ~ ~ ~ ~ ~ ~ ~ ~ ~

It was almost 6 o'clock and everyone was coming at 7:30. "It's about time we start getting ourselves ready." Rebecca said as we came in from horseback riding.

"Okay. I'll go take a shower." I said although I knew that I'd probably sweat some after the dance, but I took one anyway.

When I got out I turned on both the straightening iron and the curling iron. While they heated up I blow-dried my hair until I got it completely dry. I laughed when I looked into the mirror afterwards because my hair looked like a frizz ball. I grabbed the straightening iron and soon my hair was smooth, moisturized, and shiny.

Rebecca walked in as I finished up. "You ready for me?"

"Yep, in one second." Rebecca was going to curl my hair because she knew how to make the big spiral curls. I don't have a lot of hair so it only took her about twenty minutes to do. When she was finished, she carefully pinned my hair back and hair sprayed it so it would stay.

Once she was finished, I stepped into the gorgeous red dress and put on my flats that matched. Next, came makeup, just some blush, mascara, and a little lip gloss. When I looked into the mirror, Rebecca was crying.

"What's wrong?"

"You look so much like your mother."

I smiled trying to hold back tears but I couldn't. Her saying that set it off. Plus, I could see it in the video of my birth the night before.

"You've grown up so fast. It seems like yesterday, you were only this tall." She said putting her hand down to her knees. "You're a young woman now and you're so beautiful."

That did it.

"Now don't you start crying. Your mascara will run."

"I can't help it. With everything that's happened these past few weeks, it's hard not to get emotional."

"I know. I'm sorry." she said wiping her eyes and turning away from the mirror.

"Rebecca, you don't have to be sorry at all. You didn't do anything wrong."

"Thanks."

I smiled. When I looked at the clock it read 7:15.

Rebecca did the same. "Not much longer until everyone arrives."

"Yep."

"What do you want to do for the next fifteen minutes?"

"Well, on the day of the funeral my grandma sent me an email. It had a poem that she had gotten after mom and dad passed but I wasn't able to read it. I think now, I might be able to."

"Okay."

I headed to the computer and pulled up my emails. I opened up Grandma's email and once again read:

Gracie,

A friend of mine sent me this when your mother and father passed. It helped me a lot. I hope it helps you cope with the loss of Jason.

Love,

Grandma.

I took a deep breath and read the poem once again.

Remember me in quiet days
While raindrops whisper on your pane.
But in your memories have no grief,
Let just the joy we knew remain.

Remember me when evening stars
Look down on you with steadfast eyes.
Remember if once you wake
To catch a glimpse of red sunrise.

And when your thoughts do turn to me,
Know that I would not have you cry.
But live for me and laugh for me,
When you are happy, so am I.

Remember an old joke we shared,
Remember me when spring walks by.
Think once of me when you are glad,
And while you live, I shall not die.

Some of those things, Jason always said. Like 'I'm happy if you're happy.' He'd never want me to cry either. He always wiped my tears away. I hit reply and sent Grandma a note that read:

Dear Grandma,

Thank you so much for sending me this poem. When I first tried to read it I couldn't (of course the day of the funeral probably wasn't the best time). But, now that I read it again, it really does help a lot. I hope you have a wonderful Christmas. I love you.

Gracie.

I sat there quietly for a minute and held tight to the cross. "Jason," I whispered, "be with me now. Let your spirit run through me every step I take. Help me make you proud."

As I sat there for a few more minutes, I heard the doorbell ring. When I looked out the window I got very excited. "Rob!"

I ran outside and he was already ready for me with his arms out open wide and I jumped in his arms.

"Hey!" he exclaimed. He hugged me tight and kissed the side of my head. "You doing okay?"

I didn't answer him right away not knowing exactly what to say because one minute I would be fine and the next tears would be rolling down my cheeks. When I didn't answer, Rob's face became concerned.

Finally I said, "I'm doing better. I'm not one hundred percent and I probably won't be for a long time but, I'm getting there. I just have to take this one day at a time. You know what I mean?"

"Yeah," he smiled, "I know what you mean. Come on let's go inside." I nodded.

Soon the house was buzzing with people. Rob, Matt, and Rebecca came up to my room where I was waiting for my cue as always. Jason and I would never come out before the dance (I'm not sure why, we just never did. To be honest I thought it was a little strange but tradition is tradition I guess).

"You ready?" Rebecca asked.

"Give me ten more minutes?"

"You alright?" asked Matt.

"I'm fine." I convincingly lied.

"Okay." I didn't turn around until after they left. I didn't want them to know that I had started crying again. Especially since I wasn't sure exactly what triggered it. It was like all of a sudden I started crying. I was angry about it, too, because I thought I was doing so well.

All I thought was 'I wish all of this never would've happened' and 'I don't want to feel this way anymore, I just want Jason back.' These thoughts haunted me but I had to get rid of them because right now I had to think of Jason and how much I truly loved him. I took deep breath after deep breath and I once again heard his soft, gentle voice in my ear.

"I'm right there. Every time you put that cross around you neck, I'm right there."

I smiled. That helped more than anything ever could. Finally, I was ready to go and just in time too because there was a knock at the door.

"Come in."

"Gracie, you ready now?" asked Rebecca.

"Yeah."

"Okay." She held out her hand and I took hold of it. "Come on. Stop worrying. It'll be great."

"I know." I said looking down.

"Hey." She put her hand under my chin and lifted up my head. She looked into my eyes and said, "You can do it. You know this dance backwards and forwards. Just remember what Jason told you." She put her hand to my heart. "He's right there, always."

I held back the tears and said, "Okay, I'm ready."

Rebecca went and got everyone settled. I grabbed the cross one more time, kissed it, and whispered, "I love you Jason. This is for you."

Rebecca turned on the music and I heard the peaceful melody play. As I danced, I let the music flow through me and I relaxed just like Jason always told me to do.

As I got more and more into it, everything around me no longer existed. I was in my own world full of peace and wonder, surrounded by blues, greens, and whites. I felt as if I could fly to the heavens and be with Jason again.

I didn't want this feeling to go away. However, as soon as the music stopped I fell back into reality like a baby bird falling out of the nest a hundred feet from the ground. When I came back into focus, I looked over at Rebecca. Tears were flowing down her cheeks and it was the same story with everyone else. She immediately came over and gave me a great big hug.

Everyone began to applaud, and, as they did, Rebecca whispered in my ear. "Gracie, that was..." she stopped. She couldn't find the words but she soon did. "Amazing, phenomenal, gorgeous, passionate, full of emotion, and the absolute greatest performance I have ever seen you do. You have done Jason noble justice. No one, not even myself, could honor him as splendidly as you just did."

This time I didn't try to resist the tears. I let them freely flow down my cheeks. I didn't care about holding them back any longer.

Matt and Rob were the next to embrace me. "That was beautiful, Gracie." they said in unison.

Soon I was surrounded by everyone, something that I still wasn't quite used to. It was a little overpowering.

Rebecca could tell and she reached for my hand. "You okay?"

I took a deep breath. "Yeah, I'm okay." I said confidently. The rest of the night we ate, talked, and even laughed. It was the first time since Jason died that I truly allowed myself to let loose and be happy.

I had always thought that it was wrong to have a good time when Jason was dead. However, after I read that poem from my grandma, I realized that Jason wouldn't want me to be that way.

Jason hated sadness and despair. He said it was a waste of time. Every where he went, he brought joy, laughter, and love. It was absolutely **IMPOSSIBLE** to stay down for very long if he was around. Jason always knew the right thing to say. Whenever I had a problem, he could always help me get through it. I now knew what that line in the poem meant. "And while you live, I shall not die." It meant that even though he is no longer here in the physical sense, as long as we are happy and celebrating the Christmas season, we were keeping his spirit alive and as long as we did, he never would spiritually die.

 ~ ~ ~ ~ ~ ~ ~ ~ ~ ~

"Great night, huh?" said Rebecca after the last guest had left.

"Yeah, it really was." I hesitated a moment then said, "Didn't it almost seem like Jason wasn't gone for a minute? Especially while I danced. It was like I *was* dancing with him again."

I think she thought I was crazy because she just stared at me for a long time. But then she smiled and said, "Yes Gracie. It did. I thought I was the only one that noticed, but I guess I wasn't."

I laughed a little. "No you weren't." She started to put things away and clean up but I stopped her. "Hey, I'll do that. It's your turn to relax."

"Thanks Gracie." Although she didn't want me to know it, I could see the relief in her eyes. So, while she changed I cleaned up the food. We'd be having leftovers for a while but we don't usually mind it.

 ~ ~ ~ ~ ~ ~ ~ ~ ~ ~

Once we were comfy in our pajamas, we made some hot chocolate with marshmallows and sat and talked for hours. We talked about the night, the dance, and she told me stories about the first part of their marriage long before I came into the picture. The way they had stuck together showed me the amazing love they had for one another.

"I hope one day I can find love like that."

"You will, Gracie. Trust me, you will. Now, time to turn in. It's almost midnight. Santa won't come if we don't."

I rolled my eyes and she laughed. I knew she was kidding. She knew I didn't believe in that stuff anymore. "Alright." I said not really wanting to stop. I wanted to hear more stories and talk some more. However, she was right. It was getting late. So, we said good night and I settled into bed.

~~ ~~ ~~ ~~ ~~ ~~ ~~ ~~ ~~ ~~

I laid my head down on the big, white, fluffy pillow. As I laid there, I looked over at the picture of Jason and me last summer. It was one of my favorites. I blew him a kiss, shut off the light and gently closed my eyes.

As I drifted off to sleep I remember thinking, I wouldn't see Jason suffering tonight and I would no longer.

CHAPTER 16

Two Years Later

"Gracie Marie Anderson." called the Master of Ceremonies. I walked swiftly across the stage to receive my diploma.

"Congratulations Gracie." Mrs. Smith said as she shook my hand.

"Thank you." I replied with a smile. As I moved the tassel from left to right, I looked out into the crowd where I saw Rebecca with tears running down her face. Melissa sat next to her and the story was the same. I could see in their eyes how proud they were of me. Sometimes, it's like I can see Jason's face as if he is the one watching me and looking at me that way. Not a day goes by when I don't miss him and think of him constantly. If it weren't for the cross hanging around my neck and the DVD, I wouldn't have been able to get through the past two years nearly as easily. Although it wasn't easy anyway, just having that cross close to my heart helped.

~ ~ ~ ~ ~ ~ ~ ~ ~ ~

"Good night guys." I said as the last party guest left. It had been a great day. I got to hang with my friends one last time before we all went our separate ways as well as spend time with my family. I headed back to my room and began to pack.

"Hey, getting ready?" asked Melissa.

"Yep. You wanna help?"

"Yes, I do." she replied. I could tell that she wanted to say something, but, instead she stayed quiet. So, I finally broke the awkward silence.

"Melissa, talk to me, please. Tell me what you're thinking. You always make me tell you what I'm thinking."

"Alright. I don't want you to leave."

"I know you don't. I do love you Melissa, but, ever since mom and dad died we all knew that I really belonged with Jason and Rebecca. I never said anything about it before, but, after Jason died, things changed. Rebecca and I need each other. Besides, you'll be starting your own family before long with Eric now that he's proposed. I need to be with Rebecca."

"I know you do. Like you said, I've known it for a long time. I was just being selfish."

"No you weren't."

"Yes I was Gracie. There were a number of times when Rebecca and Jason talked to me about you coming to live with them in L.A."

"What?" I said in surprise.

"I always said no, because I didn't want to lose you."

"Melissa, you'll never lose me. It's not like I'm never gonna come visit. Besides, if I hadn't gotten into that dance program in L.A., I probably would've gone to college somewhere where I could study dance. So, I would've been leaving anyway. Just think of it this way, at least you don't have to worry about me. You know that I'm with someone who really cares about me, instead of all by myself."

She fought tears and said, "I know. I'm just gonna need some time to get used to you not living here anymore."

"You can take all the time you need." I reassured her.

～～ ～～ ～～ ～～ ～～ ～～ ～～ ～～ ～～ ～～

The next morning, I was up by six o'clock. Rebecca and Melissa were up, too. We had a four o'clock flight to L.A. (I've finally gotten used to it).

Melissa and I spent the morning and the first part of the afternoon together and we did all of our favorite things. We went to a movie, went bowling, and out for lunch. I think it made her feel better about me leaving.

~~ ~~ ~~ ~~ ~~ ~~ ~~ ~~ ~~ ~~

"Hey, Gracie wait." Melissa stopped me when we got to the gate. "You call me, okay. Call me a lot. I wanna know how you're doing."

"I promise." I replied. I gave her a hug and headed on the plane.

We put our luggage away and settled into our seats.

"Ladies and gentlemen, please fasten your seatbelts for takeoff." announced the stewardess.

Rebecca and I talked most of the way. Then, we fell asleep. I dreamed of the future. But, then again, it wasn't the true future. I was twenty-two years old and walking down the aisle, ready to get married. I heard someone quietly sobbing and felt them holding my arm. I looked up and smiled. The eyes I looked into were the eyes I had missed so much. They were Jason's.

I woke up after that feeling both happy and sad. Happy, because I had seen Jason happy, healthy, and alive. Sad, because I knew in my heart that it would never get to be that way. Jason would never be there to walk me down the aisle and cry as we danced at the reception.

As I touched the cross once again, I heard the stewardess say, "Ladies and gentlemen, if you will please once again fasten your seatbelts, we'll be landing here shortly."

Rebecca woke up and she looked at me. I smiled from ear to ear and thought to myself, 'this is it. I'm home.'

Acknowledgements

First, I'd like to thank my parents for all their support in everything I do. They've always been there for me and I appreciate everything they've done. Also to my brother who has always showed his support in everything I've ever wanted to do. To my aunt who provided her expertise in editing and helped me make it perfect. I'd also like to thank my publishing consultant, Travis Trestler for answering all my questions and helping me through the process. Thank you also to Bill Brooks who helped me find Author House and for guiding me on how to go about self-publishing this book.

About the Author

Katie Peterson was born in Leavenworth, Kansas on November 6, 1994. She is the daughter of David and Carol Peterson and she has an older brother named Patrick. She is currently a sophomore at Immaculata High School. Her interests include, singing, writing stories and songs, and spending time with her family. Katie is a baptized Catholic and is highly dedicated to her faith. She participates in her church choir and lives her life to spread God's word in any way she can. She has organized a Christian concerts with a group called "Audible Lights" to help her parish youth group attend the National Catholic Youth Conference that was held in Kansas City in November of 2009.